The Z [...] of Facts for Girls

Compiled by Joyce Parsons

Evans Brothers Limited London

Published by Evans Brothers Limited
Montague House, Russell Square,
London, E.C.1

© Evans Brothers Limited 1968
First published 1968

Set in 9/10 pt Old Style No 2 and
printed in Great Britain by Cox & Wyman Ltd.,
London, Fakenham and Reading
PB.   237   44387   2
CSD. 237   35093   9   PR. 4673

Contents

The Commonwealth

The Commonwealth as we know it today comprises the United Kingdom and over 20 independent nations together with a number of small colonies and other non-sovereign territories which are still dependent upon the UK.

This Commonwealth grew out of what used to be called the British Empire – shown as large areas of red on maps of the world printed 25 or more years ago. All the states and territories which are members of the Commonwealth (and others such as Burma and South Africa which have since left the Commonwealth) used to be governed by men sent out from the UK.

The origins of the Commonwealth date from the voyages of exploration and discovery which started at the end of the fifteenth century and continued for the next 250 years. The first explorers only made passing visits to the newly-found lands, but subsequently people from various European countries went abroad to settle permanently, sometimes seeking refuge from religious persecution. As a result of wars between the European nations, some of these settlements have been in turn colonies of several different countries.

Member countries of the British Empire such as Canada and Australia which had been settled by people of British or European stock were the first to achieve complete self-government and to be independent of the UK, while still being 'united by a common allegiance to the Crown'.

The road to independent nationhood has been a long one particularly for those countries whose populations were not predominantly of British or European descent. Once British rule was firmly established, the Governor usually sought the assistance of local leaders in running the country, some of them being appointed official advisers. Subsequently the Governor would establish a Legislative Council. At first only a few members would be elected, the remainder being appointed by the Governor, but gradually as the Council gained experience in governing the country, the people would elect more and more members.

Although the details of its power vary from colony to colony, the Legislative Council is usually only responsible for the colony's internal affairs, with the UK Parliament looking after foreign affairs. Eventually, when the Legislative Council has shown that it is able to govern the colony fairly, the country can apply to become fully independent. It can also decide whether it wishes to remain in the Commonwealth after gaining independence. Some Commonwealth countries, such as India, Pakistan and Ghana have chosen to be republics, although all Commonwealth countries recognize the Queen as Head of the Commonwealth.

The Commonwealth is a very special form of association of countries. It has no single parliament or government, no central defence force, neither has it a common foreign policy. Formal relationships within the Commonwealth depend largely upon consultation, the most important form of consultation being the Conference of Commonwealth Prime Ministers which is held at least every second year.

However, there are many informal bonds linking the member nations as a family of independent states, some of which result from the original settlers from Britain taking British culture, traditions, sports and the English language with them. So many different languages and dialects are spoken in some of the newly independent Commonwealth countries that English is the only language in which the countries' leaders can speak to their people. Imperial preferences (special reduced customs duties for the import of goods from one Commonwealth country to another) encourage trade between member nations. In the field of sport, cricket and cricketing language are familiar in Australia, England, India, New Zealand, Pakistan and the West Indies, but hardly outside the Commonwealth.

Independent Nations Within the Commonwealth

Nation	Became British Territory in*	Date of Independence†
Australia (federation of former colonies)		1901
‡Botswana (formerly Bechuanaland)	1885	1966
Canada (federation of former colonies)		1867
Ceylon	1802	1948
‡Cyprus	1878	1960
Gambia	1843	1965
‡Ghana (formerly Gold Coast)	1874	1957
‡Guyana (formerly British Guiana)	1831	1966
‡India	1757	1947
Jamaica	1655	1962
‡Kenya	1887	1963
‡Lesotho (formerly Basutoland)	1868	1966
‡Malawi (formerly Nyasaland)	1889	1964

Nation	Became British Territory in*	Date of Independence†
‡Malaysia (federation of former Malay states)		1963
Malta	1800	1964
New Zealand	1840	1907
‡Nigeria	1862	1960
‡Pakistan (formerly part of Indian Empire)		1947
Sierra Leone	1863	1961
‡Singapore	1867	1965
‡Tanzania (formerly Tanganyika and Zanzibar)	1919	1962
‡Trinidad and Tobago	1802	1962
Uganda	1888	1962
Zambia (formerly Northern Rhodesia)	1889	1964

* Dates given are either those of the commencement of continuous British rule or of the foundation of the British Crown Colony.

† Date of gaining independence of the UK. Nations which are now republics within the Commonwealth – denoted by a double dagger‡ – may have taken republican status at a later date.

Crown Colonies and Other Non-Sovereign Territories Administered by the UK

The trend towards full independent nationhood has substantially reduced the number of colonies and non-sovereign territories. Some of the countries administered by the UK listed below are well advanced in achieving self-government, while others are small island communities which would have difficulty in surviving as fully independent states.

Antigua	Dominica
Bahamas	Falkland Islands and Dependencies
Barbados	Fiji
Bermuda	Gibraltar
British Antarctic Territory	Grenada
British Honduras	Hong Kong
British Indian Ocean Territory	Mauritius
British Virgin Islands	Montserrat
Brunei	Pitcairn Islands
Cayman Islands	Rhodesia§

§ Illegally declared independent in November 1965.

St. Helena*	Swaziland
St. Kitts-Nevis	Tonga
St. Lucia	Turks and Caicos Islands
St. Vincent	Western Pacific High
Seychelles	Commission†

* Includes Ascension and Tristan da Cunha.

† Includes British Solomon Islands, Central and Southern Line Islands, Gilbert and Ellice Islands, Canton and Enderbury Islands and the Anglo-French Condominium of the New Hebrides.

The Royal Family

Queen Elizabeth II (the Queen Regnant) is the elder daughter of the late King George VI. She was born in London on April 21, 1926, and on November 20, 1947, married the *Duke of Edinburgh* (formerly Prince Philip of Greece, and a great-great-grandson of Queen Victoria). She succeeded to the Throne on the death of her father on February 6, 1952. Her Majesty has four children: *Prince of Wales* (Charles Philip Arthur George), Heir Apparent to the Throne, born on November 14, 1948; Princess Anne Elizabeth Alice Louise, born on August 15, 1950; Prince Andrew Albert Christian Edward, born on February 19, 1960, and Prince Edward Antony Richard Louis, born on March 10, 1964.

The Queen Mother is the daughter of the 14th Earl of Strathmore and Kinghorne, and was born on August 4, 1900, being given the names Elizabeth Angela Marguerite Bowes-Lyon. On April 26, 1923, she married the Duke of York, second son of King George V, and upon the abdication of King Edward VIII (now Duke of Windsor) and the accession of the Duke of York to the Throne on December 11, 1936, she became Queen. She has two children: Queen Elizabeth II (see above); and *Princess Margaret Rose*, who was born at Glamis Castle, Angus, Scotland, on August 21, 1930, and who married Mr. Anthony Charles Robert Armstrong-Jones, later created the Earl of Snowdon, on May 6, 1960. Princess Margaret has two children, David Albert Charles, Viscount Linley, born November 3, 1961, and Sarah Francis Elizabeth Armstrong-Jones, born on May 1, 1964.

Succession to the Throne

The order of succession to the Throne is now:

    Prince of Wales.

    Prince Andrew

    Prince Edward.

    Princess Anne.

Princess Margaret.
Viscount Linley.
Lady Sarah Armstrong-Jones

The Duke of Gloucester (Henry William Frederick Albert), brother of King George VI, born March 31, 1900

Prince William Henry Andrew Frederick of Gloucester, son of above, born December 18, 1941.

Prince Richard Alexander Walter George, brother of Prince William, born August 26, 1944.

Then follow Prince Edward George Nicholas Paul Patrick, the Duke of Kent (born October 9, 1935), the Duke's son Lord George Philip Nicholas Windsor (Earl of St. Andrews), the Duke's second child Lady Helen Marina Lucy Windsor, Prince Michael of Kent (born July 4, 1942), Princess Alexandra of Kent (born December 25, 1936), her son (born February 29, 1964), and her daughter (born July 31, 1966).

Monarchs of Britain

Until 1301, Wales was considered as one or more independent kingdoms having its own sovereign. In that year the son of Edward I of England was created Prince of Wales, and in 1307 he became King of England and Wales.

Before the Union of the Crowns of England and Scotland in 1603, Scotland was also an independent kingdom.

And before the year 827, England itself was not a united country, but had separate kings for such regions as Wessex, Mercia, and Northumbria. In 827 there ascended to the throne the 'first King of all the English' – Egbert the Great, King of Wessex, who subdued the other kingdoms except Northumbria and Cumbria mainly by force.

His immediate successors exercised direct rule over much of England for intermittent periods during their reigns, but England (excluding Cumbria) did not finally become a united kingdom until 954 in the reign of Edred.

In the following tables of sovereigns the dates given are those on which the respective rulers began their reigns.

English Kings (829 to 1603)

Name	Descent	Came to Throne
Saxon		
Egbert the Great		827
Ethelwulf	Son of Egbert the Great	839
Ethelbald and Ethelbert	Sons of Ethelwulf	858
Ethelred I	Third son of Ethelwulf	866
Alfred the Great	Fourth son of Ethelwulf	871
Edward the Elder	Son of Alfred the Great	901
Athelstan	First son of Edward the Elder	925
Edmund I the Elder	Third son of Edward the Elder	940
Edred	Fourth son of Edward the Elder	946
Edwy	First son of Edmund	955
Edgar the Peaceable	Second son of Edmund	959
Edward the Martyr	First son of Edgar	975
Ethelred II the Unready	Second son of Edgar	978
Edmund II (Ironside)	Third son of Ethelred	1016
Danish		
Canute	(By conquest)	1017
Harold I	Son of Canute	1035
Hardicanute	Son of Canute	1040
Saxon		
Edward the Confessor	Son of Ethelred II	1042
Harold II	Brother of Edith, wife of Edward the Confessor	1066
Norman		
William I of Normandy	(By conquest)	1066
William II	Third son of William I	1087
Henry I	Fourth son of William I	1100
Stephen	Grandson of William I	1135
Plantagenet		
Henry II	Grandson of Henry I	1154
Richard I	Third son of Henry II	1189
John	Fifth son of Henry II	1199
Henry III	Eldest son of John	1216
Edward I	Elder son of Henry III	1272

Name	Descent	Came to Throne
England and Wales		
Edward II	Fourth son of Edward I	1307
Edward III	Elder son of Edward II	1327
Richard II	Grandson of Edward III	1377
Lancaster		
Henry IV	Grandson of Edward III	1399
Henry V	Second son of Henry IV	1413
Henry VI	Son of Henry V	1422
York		
Edward IV	Great-grandson of Edward III	1461
Edward V	Elder son of Edward IV	1483
Richard III	Brother of Edward IV	1483
Tudor		
Henry VII	Son of Edmund Tudor and Margaret Beaufort, great-great-grand-daughter of Edward III	1485
Henry VIII	Second son of Henry VII	1509
Edward VI	Son of Henry VIII	1547
Jane	Grand-daughter of Mary, sister of Henry VIII	1553
Mary I	Daughter of Henry VIII	1553
Elizabeth I	Daughter of Henry VIII	1558

Kings of Great Britain (from 1603)

Stuart		
James I	(King James VI of Scotland)	1603
Charles I	Second son of James I	1625–49
(Here came Oliver Cromwell, 1653–8, and Richard Cromwell, 1658–9)		
Charles II	Second son of Charles I	1660
James II	Third son of Charles I	1685
William III	Son of William of Orange and Mary, daughter of Charles I	} 1689
Mary II	Eldest daughter of James II	
Anne	Daughter of James II	1702

Hanover

George I	Son of Ernest Augustus, First Elector of Hanover and Sophia, grand-daughter of James I	1714
George II	Son of George I	1727
George III	Grandson of George II	1760
George IV	Eldest son of George III	1820
William IV	Third son of George III	1830
Victoria	Grand-daughter of George III	1837

Saxe-Coburg

Edward VII	Eldest son of Victoria	1901

Windsor

George V	Second son of Edward VII	1910
Edward VIII	Eldest son of George V	1936
George VI	Second son of George V	1936
Elizabeth II	Elder daughter of George VI	1952

Kings of Scotland (1005 – 1603)

Malcolm II	1005	Margaret	1286–90
Duncan I	1034	John Balliol	1292–96
Macbeth	1040	Robert I (the Bruce)	1306
Malcolm III	1057	David II	1329
Donald Bane	1093	Robert II	1371
Duncan II	1094	Robert III	1390
Donald Bane (restored)	1094	James I	1406
Edgar	1097	James II	1437
Alexander I	1107	James III	1460
David I	1124	James IV	1488
Malcolm IV	1153	James V	1513
William (the Lion)	1165	Mary	1542
Alexander II	1214	James VI	1567
Alexander III	1249		

(James VI of Scotland became James I of England in 1603.)

The British Constitution

The Crown, which consists of the Queen at the head of the High Court of Parliament, is the responsible authority of Central Government. The Queen opens Parliament every year by making a speech from the Throne in the House of Lords, and thereafter she conducts the day-to-day business of State through her Privy Council. The Queen entrusts executive duties to her Ministers.

The Cabinet is formed of the Ministers of the Crown, and usually consists of 24 Ministers, not more than 22 of whom may be Members of the House of Commons. There may also be 27 Parliamentary Secretaries, of whom not more than 23 may be Members of the House of Commons, and not less than 4 must be Members of the House of Lords. The head of the Cabinet is the Prime Minister, who is appointed by the Queen.

The House of Lords consists of royal princes, archbishops, dukes, marquesses, earls, countesses in their own right, viscounts, bishops, barons, baronesses in their own right, law lords, life peers and life peeresses; it is presided over by the Lord High Chancellor. The right to sit in the House of Lords is governed by elevation to a peerage or by birth. In 1958, peeresses became eligible to sit in the House of Lords for the first time in history.

The House of Lords forms a Court of Appeal (the highest in the land), which consists of 7 law lords and some others who have held legal appointments. The decisions of this Court become law.

The House of Commons consists of 630 citizens who have been elected as Members of Parliament by their fellow-citizens. Its proceedings are governed by rules called Standing Orders, and directed by a chairman (called the Speaker) who is elected by the Members themselves. The House of Commons as elected at a General Election may continue in office for a maximum of five years, after which Parliament is declared dissolved and there has to be another General Election.

In theory no Member of the House of Commons may resign, but he must cease to be a Member when he is appointed to an office under the Crown: in order to resign he applies for the Stewardship of the Chiltern Hundreds or of the Manor of Northstead in Yorkshire. Although neither appointment carries duties or salary, it is an office under the Crown, hence anyone appointed to it is no longer allowed to be a Member.

Nearly all Members of the House of Commons belong to one or other of the political parties of the day, and when, after a General Election, one party is found to have more Members elected to the House than any other, that party forms the Government. From it the Queen appoints her Prime Minister, and the Prime Minister appoints other Ministers, some of whom form the Cabinet.

The Government will remain in office until, by vote, it is defeated in the House on some important issue; it is then called upon to resign its powers, which may be taken up by the next largest party. Alternatively, if the next party feels it is likely to be defeated by vote very soon after it forms a Government, the Prime Minister advises the Queen to dissolve Parliament, and there has to be a General Election, even if five years have not elapsed since the last General Election.

How Our Laws Are Made

One of the most important functions of Parliament is to make laws whereby the country's affairs may be regulated. While any proposed law is being discussed and shaped, it is called a Bill; when it finally receives the Queen's Assent, it becomes an Act of Parliament.

A Bill may be drafted and introduced either by the Government or by any Member of either House. Most Bills are introduced in the House of Commons, where they go through the following stages:

First Reading. The Bill is formally introduced in the House, and ordered to be printed so that everyone shall know its contents.

Second Reading. The Minister or other Member who introduced it explains the principles of the Bill and the House usually debates it and then decides, often by vote, whether it shall go any further. If the supporters of the Bill are in the majority, the Bill goes to :

Committee, where it is examined closely, clause by clause and word by word, and altered or 'amended'.

Report Stage. After the Committee has reported to the House, further amendments may be made by the House.

Third Reading. The Bill, as amended, is discussed by the House, and accepted or rejected as a whole. If it is accepted, it goes to the House of Lords, where it passes through procedure similar to that described above.

The House of Lords may accept, amend, or reject the Bill – unless it is a Finance Bill (which contains the Budget proposals) or any other Bill certified by the Speaker to be a 'Money' Bill. Since 1911, the Lords has by law had to pass such Bills without amendment.

A Bill passed by the Lords without amendment is ready for the Royal Assent, which is signified by Commissioners who act for the Queen. If it is amended it goes back to the House of Commons for the amendments to be considered; and if the Commons agrees to the amendments, the Bill is ready for the Royal Assent.

If the Lords rejects a Bill introduced in the Commons, it cannot be put forward for Royal Assent. If, however, the House of Commons passes a Bill in two successive Sessions and the House of Lords rejects it each time, the Bill goes forward for Royal Assent provided that there is a year's interval between the Second Reading in the Commons in the first Session and the Third Reading in the Commons in the second Session.

Britain's Prime Ministers
The official residence of the Prime Minister of the day is No. 10 Downing Street, just off Whitehall in London. His country residence is Chequers, near Aylesbury in Buckinghamshire.

The Prime Ministers, from Sir Robert Walpole (who is generally considered to have been the first), are as follows:

Prime Minister	Party	Date	Prime Minister	Party	Date
Sir Robert Walpole	Whig	1721	Lord North	Tory	1770
Earl of Wilmington	Whig	1742	M. of Rockingham	Whig	1782
Henry Pelham	Whig	1743	Earl of Shelburne	Whig	1782
Duke of Newcastle	Whig	1754	Duke of Portland	C.	1783
Duke of Devonshire	Whig	1756	William Pitt*	Tory	1783
Duke of Newcastle	Whig	1757	Henry Addington	Tory	1801
Earl of Bute	Tory	1762	William Pitt*	Tory	1804
George Grenville	Whig	1763	Lord Grenville	Whig	1806
Marquess of			Duke of Portland	Tory	1807
Rockingham	Whig	1765	Spencer Perceval	Tory	1809
Earl of Chatham	Whig	1766	Earl of Liverpool	Tory	1812
Duke of Grafton	Whig	1767	George Canning	Tory	1827

* William Pitt, the Younger, son of the Earl of Chatham (William Pitt, the Elder).

Prime Minister	Party	Date	Prime Minister	Party	Date
Viscount Goderich	Tory	1827	W. E. Gladstone	Lib.	1892
Duke of Wellington	Tory	1828	Earl of Rosebery	Lib.	1894
Earl Grey	Whig	1830	M. of Salisbury	Cons.	1895
Viscount Melbourne	Whig	1834	A. J. Balfour	Cons.	1902
Duke of Wellington	Tory	1834	Sir H. Campbell-		
Sir Robert Peel	Cons.	1834	Bannerman	Lib.	1905
Vct. Melbourne	Whig	1835	H. H. Asquith	Lib.-C.	1908
Sir Robert Peel	Cons.	1841	D. Lloyd George	C.	1916
Lord John Russell	Whig	1846	A. Bonar Law	Cons.	1922
Earl of Derby	Tory	1852	S. Baldwin	Cons.	1923
Earl of Aberdeen	Peelite	1852	J. R. Macdonald	Lab.	1924
Palmerston	Lib.	1855	S. Baldwin	Cons.	1924
Earl of Derby	Cons.	1858	J. R. Macdonald	Lab.-C.	1929
Vct. Palmerston	Lib.	1859	S. Baldwin	C.	1935
Earl Russell	Lib.	1865	A. N. Chamberlain	C.	1937
Earl of Derby	Cons.	1866	Winston Churchill	C.	1940
Benjamin Disraeli	Cons.	1868	C. R. Attlee	Lab.	1945
W. E. Gladstone	Lib.	1868	Sir Winston		
B. Disraeli	Cons.	1874	Churchill	Cons.	1951
W. E. Gladstone	Lib.	1880	Sir Anthony Eden	Cons.	1955
Marquess of			H. Macmillan	Cons.	1957
Salisbury	Cons.	1885	Sir Alexander		
W. E. Gladstone	Lib.	1886	Douglas-Home	Cons.	1963
M. of Salisbury	Cons.	1886	J. H. Wilson	Lab.	1964

Note: Cons. = Conservative; C. = Coalition; Lib. = Liberal; Lab. = Labour.

Highest Mountains of the UK

	County	Height (feet)
Scotland		
Ben Nevis	Inverness-shire	4,406
Ben Macdhui	Aberdeenshire/Banffshire	4,300
Braeriach	Aberdeenshire/Inverness-shire	4,248
Cairn Toul	Aberdeenshire	4,241
Cairngorm	Banffshire/Inverness-shire	4,084

	County	Height (feet)
Wales		
Snowdon	Caernarvonshire	3,560
Carnedd Llewelyn	Caernarvonshire	3,484
Carnedd Dafydd	Caernarvonshire	3,426
Glyder Fawr	Caernarvonshire	3,279
Glyder Fâch	Caernarvonshire	3,262
England		
Scafell Pike	Cumberland	3,210
Scafell	Cumberland	3,162
Helvellyn	Cumberland/Westmorland	3,118
Skiddaw	Cumberland	3,053
Bow Fell	Cumberland/Westmorland	2,960
Northern Ireland		
Slieve Donard	Co. Down	2,796

Principal Lakes of the UK

Name	County	Area (sq. miles)
Northern Ireland		
Lough Neagh	Antrim, Armagh, Down, Londonderry, Tyrone	147
Lower Lough Erne	Fermanagh	40·5
Upper Lough Erne	Cavan/Fermanagh	12·25
Scotland (freshwater, inland lochs)		
Loch Lomond	Dumbartonshire/Stirlingshire	27·5
Loch Ness	Inverness-shire	22
Loch Awe	Argyll	15
Loch Maree	Ross and Cromarty	11
Loch Morar	Inverness-shire	10·3
England		
Lake Windermere	Lancs./Westmorland	5·69
Ullswater	Cumberland/Westmorland	3·44
Bassenthwaite Water	Cumberland	2·06
Derwentwater	Cumberland	2·06
Coniston Water	Lancs.	1·89

Name	County	Area (sq. miles)
Wales		
Bala Lake	Merionethshire	3·69
Lake Vyrnwy (dammed)	Montgomeryshire	3·18

Longest Rivers of the UK

River	Source	Mouth	Length (miles)
Severn	Plinlimmon, Montgomeryshire	Bristol Channel	220
Thames	Cotswold Hills, near Cirencester, Glos.	North Sea	210
Trent	Biddulph Moor, Staffs.	Joins Yorkshire Ouse (45 miles) to form Humber (38 miles)	147
Great Ouse	Brackley, Northants.	The Wash	143
Wye	Plinlimmon, Montgomeryshire	Joins Severn near Chepstow	135
Tay	Beinn Oss, Perthshire	Firth of Tay	117
Nene	Naseby, Northants.	The Wash	100
Clyde	Earncraig, Lanarkshire	Firth of Clyde	98·5
Spey	Loch Spey, Inverness-shire	Moray Firth	98·0
Tweed	Tweedsmuir Hills, Peebleshire	North Sea	96·5

Further Reading

Children's Encyclopedia of Knowledge, Book of History (Collins).
A Pageant of History (Collins).
The Pictorial History Book (Sampson Low).
People in History, R. J. Unstead (Black).
No. 10 Downing Street: A House of History, R. J. Minney (Cassell).
Britain and Her People. A Story of a Country and its People, their history, traditions and achievements (Ward, Lock).
Scotland and Her People, Freda M. Buchanan (Lutterworth).

The World - its History and Geography

Many of the scientific and technological feats listed in this book have been achieved in the past 100 years – some, such as exploring space, in the past 10 years – yet *anthropologists*, who study how man has evolved, tell us that it has taken almost 2 million years for *Homo sapiens* to reach his present advanced state of development.

What is perhaps even more surprising is that men did not start living together in organized communities until about 6,000 years ago. If the duration of the evolution of man is likened to a single day, the earliest of all recorded civilizations, the *Egyptiac*, began at about 5 minutes to midnight. For the previous $\frac{289}{290}$ part of his life on the Earth, man led an uncivilized existence – as a savage fending only for himself and his family.

Then as climatic conditions improved with the final recession of the last ice age (about 12,000 B.C.), men gradually began to live together in tribes which in turn gradually evolved into truly civilized societies. The majority of the civilizations had their origins in river valleys.

Civilized living implies more than individuals living together and working for the benefit of the community – this is the function of the tribe. But one of the benefits of tribal living was that improved communal methods of providing food – by primitive farming rather than hunting – for the first time gave man time to spare: he no longer had to devote all his waking hours to fighting for survival.

To fill in this leisure time man developed various forms of art – drawing, sculpture, architecture, writing and music – to express his thoughts. These are among the ingredients of civilizations, each one having characteristic styles of architecture and other art forms. As civilizations developed further trade, first by barter and then for money, prospered between cities. Religion and philosophy also played an important part in all civilized societies.

The following table lists 20 principal civilizations of man. There has been a general movement of civilizations westwards from the Nile and the Euphrates-Tigris deltas, the areas which benefited first from better climates and also the build-up of fertile silt in the river deltas – factors which enabled the citizens to raise their living standards and to enjoy some leisure. The present Western civilization evolved from these earlier civilizations. However, other important civilizations evolved independently in other parts of the world.

Great Civilizations of Man

Name	Duration (approx.)	Cradle	Derivation
Egyptiac	4000 B.C.–A.D. 280	Lower Nile	Spontaneous
Sumeric	3500 B.C.–1700 B.C.	Euphrates–Tigris Delta	Spontaneous
Indic	3000 B.C.–A.D. 500	Indus and Ganges valleys	Possibly related to Sumeric
Minoan	2000 B.C.–1400 B.C.	Knossus and Crete	Spontaneous
Hittite	2000 B.C.–1200 B.C.	Turkey	Related to Minoan
Mayan	2000 B.C.–A.D. 1550	Guatemala	Spontaneous
Sinic	1600 B.C.–A.D. 220	Yellow River	Spontaneous
Babylonic	1500 B.C.–538 B.C.	Lower Mesopotamia	Related to Sumeric
Hellenic	1300 B.C.–A.D. 558	Greek mainland, Aegean Islands	Related to Minoan
Syriac	1200 B.C.–A.D. 970	Eastern Cilicia	Related to Minoan
Andean	100 B.C.–A.D. 1783	Peru	Spontaneous
Khmer	A.D. 100 –A.D. 1432	Cambodian coast	Possibly related to Indic and Sinic
Far Eastern	A.D. 589 –today	China, Japan, Korea	Related to Sinic
Western	A.D. 675 –today	Ireland	Related to Hellenic
Orthodox Christian (main)	A.D. 680 –today	Turkey	Related to Hellenic and Western
Hindu	A.D. 810 –today	Jamna-Ganges, India	Related to Indic
Orthodox Christian (Russian)	A.D. 950 –today	Upper Dnieper Basin	Related to Hellenic
Arabic	A.D. 975 –1525	Arabia, Iraq, Syria	Related to Syriac

Name	Duration (approx)	Cradle	Derivation
Mexic	A.D. 1075–1821	Mexican Plateau	Related to Mayan
Iranic	A.D. 1320–today	Oxus–Jaxartes Basin	Related to Syriac

Major Wars

It is only possible here to give the briefest outline of world history. In past centuries battles were fought in one place, after which the battle was usually named, some of the battles being isolated incidents in wars which may have lasted many years. In contrast, modern warfare tends to be much more mobile and although there were many fiercely fought engagements in the two World Wars, few can be classed as battles in the classical sense. The following list gives the dates of the more important wars.

B.C. 1200	Trojan War	1701–13	War of Spanish Succession
431–04	Peloponnesian War		
357–46	Sacred War	1740–8	War of Austrian Succession
264–41	First Punic War		
219–01	Second Punic War	1755–63	Seven Years War
149–46	Third Punic War	1773–83	American War of Independence
A.D.		1789–1815	Napoleonic Wars
1066–71	Norman Conquest of Britain	1839–41	Opium War (China)
		1853–6	Crimean War
1265–84	Conquest of Wales	1860–5	American Civil War
1290–1305	Conquest of Scotland	1898–1902	Boer War
1306–42	Scots War of Independence	1904–5	Russian–Japanese War
1336–1453	100 Years War	1914–18	World War I
1455–71	Wars of the Roses	1924	Chinese Civil War
1588–1610	Conquest of Ireland	1936–9	Spanish Civil War
1618–48	Thirty Years War	1939–45	World War II
1642–6	Civil War	1950–3	Korean War

The United Nations

The United Nations (UN) is a world organization formed to maintain peace and security for all and to provide a means of co-operation in world affairs between nations. The UN came into existence on October

24, 1945 after 51 nations had signed the *United Nations Charter*, the document which sets out its objects. Membership of the United Nations now embraces 115 sovereign states plus the two USSR republics of Byelorussia and the Ukraine.

Principal UN Organs

The General Assembly consists of all member nations of the UN, each nation having up to five representatives, but only one vote. The General Assembly meets regularly once a year in September, but special meetings may be held at any time to deal with emergencies. The Assembly has seven main committees (1) Political and Security, (2) Economic and Financial, (3) Social, Humanitarian and Cultural, (4) Trusteeship, (5) Administration and Budgetary, (6) Legal and (7) Special Political.

The Security Council is made up of eleven nations, each with one representative and one vote. There are five permanent members – China, France, UK, USA and USSR – and six members elected to serve a two-year term. The Security Council deals with problems concerning *international* peace and security. On any question before it, all permanent members must agree to the discussion; if any permanent member does not agree – i.e. uses the *veto* – the Security Council can take no action. But if the question to be discussed concerns one of the permanent members, that member is not allowed to vote.

The Economic and Social Council deals with such matters as economics, education, health and culture with particular responsibility for assisting the developing countries. It works directly to the instructions of the General Assembly and has set up commissions which investigate world conditions on the following subjects: Economics and Employment, Transport and Communications, Human Rights, Statistics, Status of Women, Drug Traffic, Population and International Commodity Trade.

The Trusteeship Council has the task of caring for territories which are placed under UN trusteeship, or for delegating that care to suitable member states. The territories cared for in this way are: New Guinea (by Australia), Nauru (Australia), Marshall Islands (USA), Marianas (USA), Caroline Islands (USA). Eight other former UN Trust Territories such as Tanganyika and Western Samoa have reached full statehood.

The International Court of Justice, comprising 15 judges from different nations, gives judgement in cases of dispute between nations. As in the case of other courts, it has a Court of Appeal (the Security Council) to which any member dissatisfied with its findings can go.

The Secretariat is the international civil service of the UN. The head of the Secretariat, appointed by the General Assembly, is known as the Secretary General. So far, three people have held this appointment:

1946–52	Trygve Lie (Norway)
1953–61	Dag Hammarskjoeld (Sweden)
1961–	U Thant (Burma)

UN Agencies
There are 15 other bodies associated with the UN which undertake special and expert work, such as:

The United Nations Educational, Scientific and Cultural Organisation (UNESCO) whose purpose is to promote education and the spread of culture among the nations so that they will understand each other better and gain the knowledge which will help them to raise their standards of living. Almost every country in the world is in membership. Headquarters: Paris.

Food and Agriculture Organisation (FAO) has the special function of helping its member nations to raise standards of food production throughout the world, improve the conditions of life of agricultural workers, and study and give information on nutrition generally. Almost every country is in membership. Headquarters: Rome.

International Civil Aviation Organisation (ICAO) helps to co-ordinate civil aircraft traffic between nations and lays down standards of safety for aircraft and standards of efficiency for crews. Headquarters: Montreal.

International Labour Organisation (ILO) studies ways of improving labour conditions, protecting foreign workers and raising the standards of living of working people everywhere. Headquarters: Geneva.

World Health Organisation (WHO) studies health and advises upon and assists in fighting disease. Headquarters: Geneva.

The Universal Postal Union (UPU), the International Telecommunication Union (ITU), the International Atomic Energy Agency (IAEA), the General Agreement on Tariffs and Trade (GATT) and the International Monetary Fund (IMF) are some of the other UN agencies.

In the UK an organization known as *The United Nations Association* (*UNA*) exists to promote the ideals of the UN. Membership is open to anybody, and members may attend meetings of local branches. Further details of UNA are available from its headquarters at 25 Charles Street, London, W.1.

Journeys of Exploration and Discovery

Date	Explorer (and Nationality)	Achievement
B.C. 450	Hanno (Carthagian)	Led 60 fifty-oared ships round the African coast as far as Sierra Leone.
330–323	Alexander the Great (Macedonian)	Marched through Persia to India and back to Babylon.
A.D. 982	Eric the Red (Viking)	Discovered Greenland.
1000	Leif Ericsson (Viking)	Reached North America (Newfoundland).
1253–5	Guillaume de Rubruquis (French)	Journeyed through Crimea, Caucasus, Asia Minor to Tripoli.
1255	Nicolo and Maffeo Polo (Venetian)	Reached Peking.
1271–94	Marco Polo (Venetian)	Journeyed through Asia.
1325–54	Ibn Batutu (Arab)	Journeyed from Tangiers via Mecca and Persia around the shores of the Indian and Pacific Oceans to China.
1300s	João Zarco and Tristão Vas (Portuguese)	Discovered Madeira and the Azores.
1487–8	Bartholomew Diaz (Portuguese)	Rounded Cape of Good Hope.
1492–6	Christopher Columbus (Italian)	Discovered San Salvador, Antigua, Bahamas, Cuba, Guadeloupe, Haiti, Jamaica, Montserrat and Puerto Rico.
1497	John Cabot (Genoese)	Discovered Cape Breton Island, Newfoundland and Nova Scotia.
1496–1503	Amerigo Vespucci (Florentine)	Explored Mexico and parts of the east coast of Central and South America.

Date	Explorer (and Nationality)	Achievement
1498	Vasco da Gama (Portuguese)	Discovered sea-route from Europe to India, round the Cape of Good Hope.
1498	Christopher Columbus (Italian)	Landed in South America.
1499	Vincente Pinzon (Portuguese)	Discovered Brazil and the Amazon.
1501–61	Various Portuguese navigators	Discovered Canton, Ceylon, Goa, Japan, Malacca and the Islands of the East Indies.
1502–4	Christopher Columbus (Italian)	Discovered Trinidad.
1509	Sebastian Cabot (Genoese)	Explored America's east coast from Florida to mouth of River Plate.
1513	Vasco Nunez de Balboa (Spanish)	Crossed Panama Isthmus and sighted Pacific Ocean.
1520	Hemàn Cortés (Spanish)	Conquered Mexico.
1519–22	Ferdinand Magellan (Portuguese)	Sailed round the World, discovering Magellan Strait and the Philippine Islands.
1534–6	Jacques Cartier (French)	Discovered Canada and explored St. Lawrence River.
1539	De Soto (Spanish)	Discovered Florida, Georgia and River Mississippi.
1554	Hugh Willoughby and Richard Chancellor (English)	Discovered the White Sea and sea-route to Russia.
1557–80	Francis Drake (English)	Sailed round the World in the *Golden Hind*.
1576	Martin Frobisher (English)	Started search for the North-West Passage to the Pacific.
1587	John Davis (English)	Discovered Davis Strait between Atlantic and Arctic Oceans.
1606	William Janszoon (Dutch)	Discovered Australia.
1606	John Smith (British)	Explored Chesapeake Bay discovering Potomac and Susquehannah.
1611	Henry Hudson (British)	Sought North-East and North-West Passages and discovered Hudson Bay, River and Strait.

Date	Explorer (and Nationality)	Achievement
1615	William Baffin (British)	Explored Baffin Bay and Baffin Island while searching for the North-West Passage.
1642–4	Abel Tasman (Dutch)	Discovered Fiji, New Zealand, Tasmania and Tonga.
1700	William Dampier (British)	Explored west coast of Australia.
1728	Vitus Bering (Danish)	Discovered Bering Strait between Asia and America.
1740–4	George Anson (British)	Sailed round the World in the *Centurion.*
1767	Samuel Wallis (British)	Discovered Tahiti.
1768–71	James Cook (British)	Sailed round the World in the *Endeavour*, charting the coast of New Zealand and the east coast of Australia.
1772–6	James Cook (British)	Discovered (in two further voyages) Cook Is., Easter Is., New Caledonia, Norfolk Is., and Hawaiian Is.
1795–7	Mungo Park (British)	Followed course of River Niger.
1821–3	James Weddell (British)	Discovered South Orkneys and Weddell Sea.
1822–5	Hugh Clapperton, Dixon Denham and Walter Oudney (British)	Expedition through Sudan to Lake Chad.
1827–8	René Caillié (French)	Crossed north-west Africa from Sierra Leone to Tangiers *via* Timbuktu.
1828–45	Charles Sturt (British)	Followed Darling and Murray Rivers and penetrated central Australia beyond Lake Eyre.
1831	James Clark Ross and John Ross (British)	Located North Magnetic Pole.
1839–43	James Clark Ross (British)	Discovered Mounts Erebus and Terror, Ross Ice Barrier and Victoria Land (Antarctica).
1849–73	David Livingstone (British)	Followed the course of the River Zambesi and discovered Victoria Falls and Lake Nyasa.
1856	John Speke (British)	Discovered Lake Tanganyika.

Date	Explorer (and Nationality)	Achievement
1858	John Speke (British)	Discovered Lake Victoria Nyanza.
1862	John Speke and J. A. Grant (British)	Discovered source of the White Nile.
1864	Samuel Baker (British)	Discovered Lake Albert Nyanza.
1869–74	Gustav Nachtigal (German)	Crossed North Africa from Tripoli, *via* Fezzan and Bornu to Cairo.
1870–2	Henry Stanley (British)	Met and explored with David Livingstone.
1872–4	Julius von Payer and K. Weyfrecht (Bohemian)	Discovered Franz Josef Land.
1874–7	Henry Stanley (British)	Followed course of River Congo.
1890–1909	Sven Hedin (Swedish)	Journeyed through Central Asia to Tibet and China.
1901	Robert Falcon Scott (British)	Discovered King Edward VII Land.
1903–6	Roald Amundsen (Norwegian)	First navigated the North-West Passage.
1909	Robert Peary (US)	Reached North Pole.
1911	Roald Amundsen (Norwegian)	Reached South Pole (Dec. 14).
1912	Robert Falcon Scott (British)	Reached South Pole (Jan. 18).
1953	Edmund Hillary (New Zealander) & Sherpa Tensing (Nepalese)	Climbed Mount Everest.
1957–8	Vivian Fuchs (British) & Edmund Hillary (New Zealander)	Crossed Antarctic continent *via* South Pole.
1961–2	Yuri Gagarin & Gherman Titov (Russian), Alan Shepard, Virgil Grissom & John Glenn (US)	First journeys into space.

The World's Continents and Oceans

The total area of the surface of the Earth is about 197 million square miles, of which water covers about 139·1 million square miles or more accurately 70·8 per cent.

The Continents

The Earth's land surface embraces seven continents with their associated islands. By definition a continent is a large land mass, not broken by a large stretch of sea, so Europe, Africa and Asia are physically, though not politically, one continent known as Afro-Euroasia. Oceania includes Australia, New Zealand and the non-Asia Pacific Islands. The sizes and populations of the continents in millions are shown below:

Continent	Sq. miles	Populations
Europe	4·1 m.*	449 m.†
Asia	17·0 m.	1,855 m.†
Russia	—	233·5 m.
North and Central America	9·3 m.	296 m.
South America	6·8 m.	172 m.
Africa	11·7 m.	319 m.
Oceania	3·2 m.	18 m.
Antarctica	5·2 m.	—
Total	51·0 m.	3,342 m.

* Including 2·2 m. sq. miles of USSR territory west of the Ural Mountains.
† Excluding USSR.

The Oceans and Great Seas

The three oceans (Atlantic, Indian and Pacific) of the World, together with the Arctic Sea form one vast mass of water. *Seas* are smaller, more self-contained portions of the oceans, such as the Mediterranean Sea, which is almost entirely surrounded by land. If the adjacent seas are detached, and the Arctic Sea regarded as an ocean, the ocean areas in millions of square miles, are:

Atlantic	31·8
Pacific	63·8
Indian	28·3
Arctic	5·4
Other Seas (see p. 37)	9·8
Total	139·1

Nations of the World and their Capitals

Country	Capital City	Country	Capital City
Europe		USSR (Europe)	Moscow
Albania	Tirana	Byelorussia	Minsk
Andorra	Andorra LaVella	Estonia	Tallinn
Austria	Vienna	Latvia	Riga
Belgium	Brussels	Lithuania	Vilnius
Bulgaria	Sofia	Moldavia	Kishinev
Cyprus	Nicosia	RSFSR	
Czechoslovakia	Prague	(Europe)	Moscow
Denmark	Copenhagen	Ukraine	Kiev
Finland	Helsinki	Vatican	Vatican City
France	Paris	Yugoslavia	Belgrade
Germany, West	Bonn		
East	E. Berlin	**Asia**	
Gibraltar	Gibraltar	Aden	Aden
Greece	Athens	Afghanistan	Kabul
Hungary	Budapest	Bahrain	Manama
Iceland	Reykjavik	Bhutan	Punakha
Irish Republic	Dublin	Brunei	Brunei Town
Italy	Rome	Burma	Rangoon
Liechtenstein	Vaduz	Cambodia	Phnom Penh
Luxembourg	Luxembourg	Ceylon	Colombo
Malta	Valletta	China, Mainland	Peking
Monaco	Monaco-Ville	Taiwan	
Netherlands	Amsterdam	(Formosa)	T'aipei
Norway	Oslo	Hong Kong	Victoria
Poland	Warsaw	India	New Delhi
Portugal	Lisbon	Indonesia	Djakarta
Rumania	Bucharest	Iran (Persia)	Teheran
San Marino	San Marino	Iraq	Baghdad
Spain	Madrid	Israel	Jerusalem
Sweden	Stockholm	Japan	Tokyo
Switzerland	Berne	Jordan	Amman
United Kingdom	London-	Korea, North	P'yongyang
England	London	South	Seoul
Wales	Cardiff	Kuwait	Kuwait City
Scotland	Edinburgh	Laos	Vientaine
N. Ireland	Belfast	Lebanon	Beirut
Isle of Man	Douglas	Malaysia	Kuala Lumpur
Jersey	St. Helier	Malaya	Kuala Lumpur
Guernsey	St. Peter Port	Sabah	Jesselton

Country	Capital City	Country	Capital City
Sarawak	Kuching	Burundi	Bujumbura
Maldive Is.	Malé	Cameroon	Yaoundé
Mongolia	Ulaan Baatar	Cape Verde Is.	Praia
Muscat and		Central African	
Oman	Muscat	Republic	Bangui
Nepal	Katmandu	Chad	Fort-Lamy
Pakistan	Rawalpindi	Comoro Is.	Moroni
Philippine Is.	Quezon City	Congo Republic	Kinshasa
Qatar	Doha	Congo	Brazzaville
Ryukyu Is.	Naha City	Dahomey	Porto-Novo
Saudi Arabia	Riyadh	Ethiopia and	
Sikkim	Gangtok	Eritrea	Addis Ababa
Singapore	Singapore City	French	
Syria	Damascus	Somaliland	Djibouti
Thailand	Bangkok	Gaboon	Libreville
Timor	Dili	Gambia	Bathurst
Trucial Oman	Dubai	Ghana	Accra
Turkey	Ankara	Guinea	Conakry
USSR (Asia)	Moscow	Ifní	Sidi Ifní
Armenia	Yerevan	Ivory Coast	Abidjan
Azerbaydzhan	Baku	Kenya	Nairobi
Georgia	Tbilisi	Lesotho	
Kazakhstan	Alma Ata	(Basutoland)	Maseru
Kirghizia	Frunze	Liberia	Monrovia
RSFSR (Asia)	Moscow	Libya	Tripoli,
Tadzhikstan	Dushanbe		Benghazi
Turkmemstan	Ashkhabad	Madagascar	
Uzbekistan	Tashkent	(Malagasy	
Vietnam, North	Hanoi	Republic)	Tananarive
South	Saigon	Malawi	
Yemen	Taiz	(Nyasaland)	Zomba
		Mali	Bamako
Africa		Mauritania	Nouakchott
Algeria	Algiers	Mauritius	Port Louis
Angola	São Paulo de	Morocco	Rabat
	Luanda	Mozambique	Lourenço
Ascension Is.	Georgetown		Marques
British Indian	Mahé,	Niger	Niamey
Ocean Territory	Seychelles	Nigeria	Lagos
Botswana		Portuguese	
(Bechuanaland)	Gaberones	Guinea	Bissau

Country	Capital City
La Réunion	St. Denis
Rhodesia	Salisbury
Rwanda	Kigali
St. Helena	Jamestown
São Tomé and Principé	São Tomé
Sénégal	Dakar
Seychelles	Port Victoria
Sierra Leone	Freetown
Somalia	Mogadishu
South Africa	Pretoria, Cape Town
South West Africa	Windhoek
Spanish Guinea	Santa Isabel
Spanish Sahara	El Aiun
The Sudan	Khartoum
Swaziland	Mbabane
Tanzania (Tanganyika and Zanzibar)	Dar es Salaam
Togo	Lomé
Tristan da Cunha	Edinburgh
Tunisia	Tunis
Uganda	Kampala
United Arab Republic	Cairo
Upper Volta	Ouagadougou
Zambia (Northern Rhodesia)	Lusaka

North and Central America

Country	Capital City
Antigua	St. Johns
Bahamas	Nassau
Barbados	Bridgetown
Bermuda	Hamilton
Brit. Honduras	Belize
Canada	Ottawa
Cayman Is.	Georgetown
Costa Rica	San José
Cuba	Havana

Country	Capital City
Dominica	Roseau
Dominican Republic	Santo Domingo
El Salvador	San Salvador
Greenland	Godthaab
Grenada	St. George's
Guadeloupe	Point à Pitre
Guatemala	Guatemala City
Haiti	Port-au-Prince
Honduras	Tegucigalpa
Jamaica	Kingston
Martinique	Fort de France
Mexico	Mexico City
Montserrat	Plymouth
Netherlands Antilles	Willemstad
Nicaragua	Managua
Panama	Panama City
Panama Canal Zone	Balboa
Puerto Rico	San Juan
St. Pierre and Miquelon	St. Pierre
St. Kitts-Nevis-Anguilla	Basseterre
St. Lucia	Castries
St. Vincent	Kingstown
Trinidad and Tobago	Port-of-Spain
Turks and Caicos Is.	Grand Turk
United States of America	Washington, DC
Virgin Is. (British)	Road Town
(US)	Charlotte Amalie

South America

Country	Capital City
Argentina	Buenos Aires
Bolivia	La Paz

Country	Capital City	Country	Capital City
Brazil	Brasília	French Polynesia	Papeete
Chile	Santiago	Gilbert and Ellice Is.	Tarawa
Colombia	Bogotà	Guam	Agana
Ecuador	Quito	Hawaii	Honolulu
Falkland Is.	Port Stanley	Nauru	Nauru
French Guinea	Cayenne	New Caledonia	Nouméa
Guyana	Georgetown	New Hebrides	Vila
Paraguay	Asunción	New Zealand	Wellington
Peru	Lima	Niue	Alofi
Surinam	Paramaribo	Papua and New Guinea	Port Moresby
Uruguay	Montevideo	Pitcairn Is.	Adamstown
Venezuela	Caracas	Samoa, Eastern	Pago-Pago
		Western	Apia
Oceania		Tokelau Is.	—
Australia	Canberra	Tonga	Nuku'alofa
British Solomon Is.	Honiara		
Cook Islands	Avarua		
Fiji	Suva		

Largest Cities of the World

Populations in the following list are given to the nearest tenth of a million and are only approximate. City populations change, usually upwards, partly because of natural increase but also through city boundaries being altered.

City (and Country)	Population (m.)	City (and Country)	Population (m.)
Tokyo (Japan)	10·9	Chicago (USA)	3·6
New York (USA)	8·1	Rio de Janeiro (Brazil)	3·6
London (UK)	7·9	Cairo (UAR)	3·5
Buenos Aires (Argentina)	7·0	Berlin (Germany)	3·3
Shanghai (China)	6·9	Osaka (Japan)	3·2
Moscow (USSR)	6·5	Tientsin (China)	3·2
Mexico City (Mexico)	5·3	Seoul (South Korea)	3·0
Calcutta (India)	4·6	Djakarta (Indonesia)	2·9
Bombay (India)	4·5	Paris (France)	2·8
São Paulo (Brazil)	4·5	Madrid (Spain)	2·6
Peking (China)	4·0	Los Angeles (USA)	2·5
Leningrad (USSR)	3·7	Rome (Italy)	2·5

City (and Country)	Popula-tion (m.)	City (and Country)	Popula-tion (m.)
Shenyang (China)	2·4	Philadelphia (USA)	2·1
Sydney (Australia)	2·3	Melbourne (Australia)	2·1
Chungking (China)	2·1	Wuhan (China)	2·1

Largest Islands

Island	Ocean	Area (sq. miles)
Australia	Pacific	2,948,000
Greenland	Arctic	840,000
New Guinea	Pacific	317,000
Borneo	Indian	287,000
Baffin Land	Arctic	235,000
Madagascar	Indian	228,800
Sumatra	Indian	163,000
Honshu, Japan	Pacific	88,500
Great Britain	North Atlantic	84,186
Ellesmere Island	Arctic	82,100
Victoria Island	Arctic	81,900
Celebes	India	73,000
South Island, New Zealand	Pacific	58,093
Java	Indian	48,600
North Island, New Zealand	Pacific	44,281
Cuba	Atlantic	44,200
Newfoundland	North Atlantic	42,734
Luzon, Philippines	Pacific	41,000
Iceland	North Atlantic	39,700
Mindanao, Philippines	Pacific	37,000
Hokkaido, Japan	Pacific	34,700
Novaya Zemlya	Arctic	32,000
Ireland	North Atlantic	31,839
Hispaniola	Atlantic	29,530
Sakhalin,	Pacific	29,100
Tasmania	Pacific	26,215
Ceylon	Indian	25,400

Highest Mountains

Name	Range	Height (feet)
Everest	Himalayas	29,028
Godwin Austen (K2)	Karakoram	28,250

Name	Range	Height (feet)
Kangchenjunga I	Himalayas	28,208
Lhotse I	Himalayas	27,923
Makalu I	Himalayas	27,824
Dhaulagiri I	Himalayas	26,810
Manaslu I	Himalayas	26,760
Cho Oyu	Himalayas	26,750
Nanga Parbat	Himalayas	26,660
Annapurna I	Himalayas	26,504
Gasherbrum I	Karakoram	26,470
Broad Peak I	Karakoram	26,400
Gasherbrum II	Karakoram	26,360
Shisha Pangma	Himalayas	26,291
Gasherbrum III	Karakoram	26,090
Annapurna II	Himalayas	26,041
Gasherbrum IV	Karakoram	26,000

Active Volcanoes

Name	Range (or Country)	Height (feet)
Guallatiri	Andes	19,882
Lascar	Andes	19,652
Cotopaxi	Andes	19,347
Tupungatito	Andes	18,504
Popocatépetl	Altiplano de Mexico	17,887
Sangay	Andes	17,749
Tungurahua	Andes	16,512
Cotacachi	Andes	16,197
Purace	Andes	15,604
Klyvuchevskaya	Sredinnyy Khrebet	15,584
Wrangell	Alaska	14,005
Tajumulco	(Guatemala)	13,812
Mauna Loa	(Hawaii)	13,680
Cameroon Mountain	(Cameroon)	13,350

Highest and Lowest Points in Each Continent

Continent	Highest Point	Country	Height (feet)
Africa	Mt. Kilimanjaro	Tanzania	19,340
N. America	Mt. McKinley	Alaska	20,320
S. America	Cerro Aconcagua	Argentina	22,834
Antarctica	Vinson Massif	Sentinel Range	16,860

Asia	Everest	Nepal–Tibet	29,028
Europe	Mt. El'brus	USSR	18,481
Oceania	Mt. Sukarno	New Guinea	17,096

Continent	Lowest Point	Country	Depth below Sea Level
Africa	Munkhafad el Qattâra	Egypt	436
N. America	Death Valley	USA	282
S. America	Rio Negro	Argentina	98
Antarctica		Marie Byrd Land	8,100 (ice-filled)
Asia	Dead Sea	Jordan	1,286
Europe	Zuider Zee	Netherlands	16
Oceania	Lake Eyre	Australia	38

Ocean Deeps

Name	Ocean	Greatest Depth (feet)
Mariana Trench	West Pacific	35,760
Tonga-Kermadec Trench	South Pacific	35,598
Philippine Trench	West Pacific	34,578
Kuril-Kamchatka Trench	West Pacific	34,062
Japan Trench	West Pacific	34,038
Solomon Trench	South Pacific	29,988
Puerto Rico Trench	West Atlantic	27,498
South Sandwich Trench	South Atlantic	27,112
Diamantina Trench	Indian	26,400
Yap Trench	West Pacific	26,280
Peru–Chile Trench*	East Pacific	26,160
Aleutian Trench	North Pacific	25,194
Romanche Trench	Atlantic	25,050

* This is believed to be the longest deep sea trench extending for some 2,200 miles.

Inland Seas and Lakes

Name	Location	Area (sq. miles)
Malay Sea	Far East	3,144,000
Caribbean Sea	West Indies	1,063,000
Mediterranean Sea	Europe, Africa	967,000
Bering Sea	Alaska, Siberia	876,000

Name	Location	Area (Sq. miles)
Gulf of Mexico	North America	596,000
Sea of Okhotsk	East Siberia	590,000
East China Sea	Far East	482,000
Hudson Bay	Canada	476,000
Sea of Japan	Far East	389,000
Andaman Sea	Burma	308,000
North Sea	NW Europe	222,000
Black Sea	Russia, Turkey	178,000
Caspian Sea	Russia, Iran	170,000
Red Sea	Africa, Arabia	169,000
Baltic Sea	Scandinavia	163,000
Persian Gulf	Persia	92,200
Gulf of St. Lawrence	Canada	91,800
Lake Superior	Canada	31,820
Lake Victoria Nyanza	Africa	26,300
Aral Sea	Kazakhstan	26,200
Lake Huron	Canada, USA	23,010
Lake Michigan	USA	22,400
Lake Baikal	Siberia	13,200
Lake Tanganyika	Africa	12,700
Great Bear Lake	Canada	12,200
Great Slave Lake	Canada	11,200
Lake Malawi	Africa	11,000

Longest Rivers

Name	Location	Length (miles)
Nile	North Africa	4,145
Amazon	South America	3,910
Mississippi–Missouri	USA	3,710
Yenisey-Angara-Selenga	USSR	3,690
Ob-Irtysh	USSR	3,460
Yangtse Kiang	China	3,400
Hwang Ho (Yellow River)	China	3,000
Congo	Central Africa	2,720
Amur-Argun	China	2,700
Lena-Kirenga	Central Siberia	2,650
Mackenzie-Peace	Canada	2,630
Mekong	Asia	2,600

Name	Location	Length (miles)
Niger	West Africa	2,600
La Plata Paranà	South America	2,500
Murray-Darling	Australia	2,300
Volga	USSR	2,290

Great Waterfalls – by height

Name	River	Location	Height (feet)
Angel	Carrao	Venezuela	3,212
Tugela	Tugela	Natal	3,110
Utigård	Jöstedal Glacier	Norway	2,625
Mongefossen	Monge	Norway	2,540
Yosemite	Yosemite Creek	USA	2,425
Østre Mardøla Foss	Mardals	Norway	2,154
Tyssestrengane	Tysso	Norway	2,120
Kukenaom	Arabopó	Venezuela	2,000
Sutherland	Arthur	New Zealand	1,904
Kjellfossen	Naeröfjord feeder	Norway	1,841
Ribbon	Ribbon Fall Stream	USA	1,612
King George VI	Utshi	Guyana	1,600
Wollomombi	Wollomombi	Australia	1,580
Roraima	Mazaruni	Guyana	1,500

Great Waterfalls – by volume

Name	River	Mean Annual Flow (cu. ft. per sec.)	Height (feet)
Stanley	Congo	600,000	200
Guaíra	Alto Paraná	470,000	374
Khône	Mekong	410,000	70
Niagara	Niagara	212,000	167
Paulo Afonso	São Francisco	100,000	192
Uruburpunga	Alto Paraná	97,000	40
Cataratas del Iguazú	Iguazú	61,660	308
Patos-Maribondo	Rio Grande	53,000	115
Victoria	Zambezi	38,430	355
Grand	Hamilton	35,000	245
Kaieteur	Potaro	23,400	741

Longest Glaciers

Name	Length (miles)
Lambert–Fisher Ice Passage, Antarctica	320
Novaya Zemlya, North Island, USSR	260
Arctic Institute Ice Passage, Victoria Land, Antarctica	225
Nimrod–Lennox–King Ice Passage, Antarctica	180
Denman Glacier, Antarctica	150
Beardmore Glacier, Antarctica	140
Recovery Glacier, Antarctica	140
Petermanns Gletscher, Knud Rasmussen Land, Greenland	124
Un-named Glacier, Ross Ice Shelf, Antarctica	120
Slessor Glacier, Antarctica	115

Principal Deserts

Name	Countries	Area (sq. miles)
Sahara	Algeria, Chad, Egypt, Libya, Mali, Mauritania, Morocco, Niger, Spanish Sahara, Sudan, Tunisia	3,250,000
Australian	Australia	600,000
Arabian	Saudi Arabia, People's Republic of South Yemen, Yemen	500,000
Gobi	Inner and Outer Mongolia	400,000
Kalahari	Botswana	200,000
Takla Makan	Sinkiang, China	125,000
Kara Kum	Turkmenistan, USSR	105,000
Thar	India, West Pakistan	100,000

Seven Wonders of the World

The Seven Wonders of Antiquity: 1, The Pyramids of Giza, Egypt: 2, The Hanging Gardens of Semiramis, Babylon, Iraq; 3, The Tomb of King Mausolus of Caria (Halicarnassus, Turkey); 4, The Temple of Diana (Ephesus, Turkey); 5, The Statue of Apollo or Colossus of Rhodes; 6, The Statue of Jupiter (Olympia, Greece); 7, The Lighthouse on Pharos near Alexandria, Egypt.

The Seven Wonders of the Middle Ages: 1, Colosseum of Rome; 2, The Catacombs of Alexandria; 3, The Great Wall of China; 4, Stonehenge;

5, The Leaning Tower of Pisa; 6, The Porcelain Tower of Nanking; 7, The Mosque of St. Sophia (Constantinople, now Istanbul).

The Seven Natural Wonders of the World: 1, The Grand Canyon, Colorado River, Arizona; 2, Rio de Janeiro Harbour, Brazil; 3, Iguazu Falls, Argentina; 4, Yosemite Valley and the Giant Sequocas of California; 5, Mount Everest; 6, The River Nile; 7, The Northern Lights (*Aurora borealis*).

Principal Religions of the World

Christian –		
Roman Catholic	550	*(million members)*
Eastern Orthodox	137	
Protestant	216	
	—	
Total	903	
Moslem	433	
Hindu	335	
Confucian	300	
Buddhist	153	
Shinto	51	
Taoist	50	
Jewish	13	

Principal Languages of the World

	(millions)		*(millions)*
Mandarin Chinese	550	Urdu (Pakistan, India)	56
English	305	Cantonese (China)	50
Russian	180	Javanese (Indonesia)	45
Hindi	175	Telugu (India)	45
Spanish	170	Ukrainian	42
German	122	Korean	40
Japanese	100	Min (China)	40
Arabic	90	Tamil (India, Ceylon)	40
Bengali (India, Pakistan)	90	Wu (China)	40
Portuguese	90	Marathi	37
Malay	75	Korean	35
French	73	Polish	34
Italian	60		

Probably more than 2,000 languages are spoken today, many by single tribes and other comparatively small groups. Details of many of these languages have not even been recorded. The 25 languages listed on page 41 account for over 80 per cent of the world's population.

Calendars of the World

The Roman Calendar was devised from one supposed to have been invented by Romulus who, according to mythology, founded the city of Rome in 753 B.C. The first Roman year was of 304 days divided into 10 months. Later two more months were added and the year then consisted of 12 months of 29 and 30 days alternately, plus an extra day, making 355 days in all. Since this arrangement did not coincide with a true year (one complete revolution of the Earth round the Sun), the Roman Calendar resulted in much confusion after some hundreds of years, and it gave way to the Julian Calendar.

The Julian Calendar was worked out by Sosigenes, an Egyptian astronomer, and introduced by Julius Caesar in 45 B.C. It fixed the average length of the year at $365\frac{1}{4}$ days, which resulted in a loss of 11 minutes 10 seconds every year. This loss mounted as hundreds of years went by, again resulting in confusion.

The Gregorian Calendar eventually put the matter right, and it is the Calendar used by nearly all the world today. It was introduced by Pope Gregory XIII in 1582, and established the year at 365 days 5 hours 49 minutes 12 seconds. England did not adopt the Calendar until 1752, by which time the reckoning by the old Calendar was 11 days too short; thus, when the Gregorian Calendar came into force, 11 days had to be dropped altogether. This led to some trouble because many people thought that they were being robbed of 11 days of life; but eventually everybody settled down to the new way of reckoning.

Leap Year. Our present ordinary calendar year consists of 365 days, with the Leap Year of 366 days accounting for the odd hours, minutes, and seconds. Leap years fall every fourth year, in years which can be divided by 4, except that unless century-years (*i.e.* 1800, 1900, 2000) can be divided by 400 they are not considered as Leap Years.

There are other Calendars which are used for special purposes side by side with the Gregorian Calendar. These are:

The Jewish Calendar, which is calculated from the supposed date of the Creation (set at 3,760 years and 3 months before the birth of Christ). The ordinary Jewish year has 353, 354 or 355 days, and is made up of 12 months. However, to bring the Jewish Calendar into line with the solar year a 13th month is added in some years. The Jewish months have 30 and 29 days alternately, and are called Tishri, Hesvan, Kislev, Tebet, Sebat, Adar, Nisan, Yiar, Sivan, Tamuz, Ab, and Elul; in 13 month years (of 383, 384, or 385 days) an extra 30-day month called Veadar, is inserted after Adar. The Jewish New Year's Day comes some time between September 5 and October 5 in the Gregorian Calendar.

The Mohammedan Calendar is used in some parts of India, Malaysia, Arabia, Iraq, and Egypt, and is reckoned from the flight of Mohammed from Mecca to Medina on July 16 A.D. 622 (called the Hejira). The Moslem year has an average length of 354 days 8 hours 48 minutes, and is divided into 12 months of 30 and 29 days alternately. There is a cycle of 30 years, 19 of which have 354 days and 11 have 355 days, the extra day being added to the last month of the year. Since this method of calculation does not correspond to the solar year, months and seasons correspond only once in 34 Mohammedan years, which period is almost exactly equivalent to 33 solar years.

The Coptic Calendar is used by people in parts of Ethiopia and Egypt, and is of 365 days made up of 12 months of 30 days each plus 5 extra (holiday) days for 3 years and 6 extra days for every 4th (Leap) year.

Dates to Remember Each Year

Movable
Easter Day can fall at any time between March 22 and April 25, it being fixed as the first Sunday after the full moon which happens on or immediately after March 21. Maundy Thursday is the Thursday and Good Friday is the Friday before Easter Day, and the day following Easter Day is a Bank Holiday. Shrove Tuesday (Pancake Day) is the Tuesday and Ash Wednesday is the Wednesday in the seventh week before Easter.

Whit Sunday is the seventh Sunday after Easter, and the day following it was formerly Bank Holiday. Whit Sunday falls between May 10 and June 13. As from 1967 the Whit Monday Bank Holiday has been replaced by the Late Spring Holiday, the date of which is fixed by Parliament. It will be on the last Monday of May in 1969 and 1970.

August Bank Holiday was traditionally the first Monday in August, but since 1966 it has been replaced by the Late Summer Holiday on either the last Monday of August or the first in September. At the time of going to press the following dates have been announced: 1969 – September 1, 1970 – August 31.

In some towns and regions (notably Scotland and Northern Ireland) the dates of Bank Holidays are varied by local agreement, particularly if they conflict with local holiday weeks.

Fixed

Jan. 1 – New Year's Day
26 – Foundation Day
(Australia)
Feb. 6 – New Zealand Day
14 – St. Valentine's Day
Mar. 1 – St. David's Day
17 – St. Patrick's Day
Apl. 1 – All Fools' Day
21 – The Queen's Birthday
23 – St. George's Day
May 24 – Commonwealth Day
Jun. 2 – Coronation Day (1953)
10 – Prince Philip's Birthday
Jul. 1 – Canada Day

Jul. 4 – Independence Day
(USA)
Aug. 4 – Queen Mother's
Birthday
Oct. 21 – Trafalgar Day
24 – United Nations
Founded (1945)
31 – All Hallow's Eve
Nov. 14 – Prince of Wales's
Birthday
30 – St. Andrew's Day
Dec. 25 – Christmas Day
26 – Boxing Day
31 – New Year's Eve

International Date Line

Places east of Greenwich have times which are fast of Greenwich Mean Time, and places west have times which are slow, the difference being 1 hour for each 15° of longitude (see *World Times at Greenwich Noon* on page 46).

On the other side of the world, crossing the Pacific from north to south, there is the meridian of 180° longitude, and it is here that two adjacent days of the calendar meet.

Thus, if two travellers can go so fast that they can reach the 180° meridian from Greenwich in a few seconds, and both start off in opposite directions at midnight on a Thursday, then the one who goes westward (across the Atlantic) will go backwards in time and arrive at 180° some 12 hours earlier by local time; that is, at about noon on Thursday. The other, going eastwards (across Europe and Russia), will go ahead of time and arrive at the same spot some 12 hours later by local time; that is, at noon on Friday. Although they have taken but a few seconds on their respective journeys, there is a day difference between them by calendar when they arrive. Hence it is said that adjacent days meet at 180° longitude.

So that there should be no muddle over this, an International Date Line has been established. For most of its length it follows the 180° meridian, but it varies slightly so that it runs through the middle of the Bering Strait, then to the east of the Aleutian Islands; later it goes westwards of the Fiji, Tonga, and Chatham Islands.

A captain of a ship or aircraft crossing the Date Line puts his calendar back a day when going in an easterly direction, and forward a day when going in a westerly direction.

Summer Time
In Britain, the idea of putting the clock forward one hour during the summer months first took effect in 1916 (during World War I). The purpose of this arrangement was at first to save power for lighting, and later (in peacetime) to enable people to enjoy longer summer evenings in the open.

As an experiment Summer Time will extend throughout the year in the UK from the day in the early spring of 1968 when the clocks were put forward one hour. This will mean that the time in the UK will be the same as in the majority of west European countries all the year round. Central European Time is one hour fast of Greenwich Mean Time.

Other places adopt systems of Summer Time. Amongst these are: Albania, Azores, Bahamas, British Honduras, Canada (Yukon excepted), China (parts only), Dominican Republic, Formosa, Hong Kong, Iceland, Irish Republic, Italy, Macao, Madeira, Norway, Poland, Portugal, USA (parts only), Syria, Turkey, United Arab Republic, Uruguay.

World Times at Greenwich Noon

Nearly all places in the world have two times – local standard time (which is the time shown on local clocks) and longitude time (the time worked out at the rate of one hour for each 15 degrees of longitude east or west of Greenwich).

The second kind of time is useful mainly to sailors and airmen, who have to know about longitude in order to fix their positions when making voyages and flights. It would not be convenient to use this kind of time on land.

For example, when it is noon at Greenwich it is only 11.40 a.m. (20 minutes earlier) at Falmouth by longitude time. The Falmouth clocks would show noon, however, and so would the clocks in every other place in the UK, no matter what its longitude. Thus there is no muddle over time in places within the country which are only a few miles apart.

But the UK is small compared with some countries. In the USA, for example, the country is divided into time-zones, and when it is 7 a.m. in New York by the clocks, it is only 4 a.m. in San Francisco (three hours earlier).

The table shows the principal cities of the world in the first column, the local standard (clock) time in the second, and the longitude time in the third, when it is noon at Greenwich. The 24-hour clock is used, and figures less than 12 are a.m., while figures more than 12 are p.m.

Adelaide	21.30	21.14	Bucharest	14.00	13.45
Aden	15.00	13.1	Buenos Aires	9.00	8.7
Algiers	12.00	12.12	Cairo	14.00	14.5
Amsterdam	13.00	12.19	Calcutta	17.30	17.53
Athens	14.00	13.33	Canton	20.00	19.33
Baltimore	7.00	6.44	Cape Town	14.00	13.13
Belfast	13.00	11.35	Chicago	6.00	6.10
Berlin	13.00	12.54	Colombo	17.30	17.13
Berne	13.00	12.30	Concepcion (Chile)	7.00	7.8
Bombay	17.30	16.51	Constantinople	14.00	13.56
Boston	7.00	7.15	Copenhagen	13.00	12.50
Brindisi	13.00	13.12	Dublin	12.00	11.35
Brisbane	22.00	22.13	Durban	14.00	14.2
Brussels	13.00	12.18	Edinburgh	13.00	11.48

Genoa	13.00	12.36	Odessa	15.00	14.1
Gibraltar	13.00	11.29	Oslo	13.00	12.40
Guatemala	6.00	5.58	Panama	7.00	6.42
Halifax, Nova Scotia	8.00	7.45	Paris	13.00	12.10
Hamburg	13.00	12.40	Peking	20.00	20.46
Havana	7.00	6.30	Penang	20.00	18.42
Hobart	22.00	21.48	Perth, W.A.	20.00	19.40
Hong Kong	20.00	19.35	Pretoria	14.00	13.54
Honolulu	2.00	1.20	Quebec	7.00	7.15
Karachi	17.00	16.28	Rangoon	18.30	18.20
Kingston, Jamaica	7.00	6.55	Rio de Janeiro	9.00	9.8
Leningrad	15.00	14.1	Rome	13.00	12.50
Lima	7.00	6.52	Salonica	14.00	13.32
Lisbon	12.00	11.24	San Francisco	4.00	3.50
London	13.00	12.00	Santiago	8.00	7.20
Los Angeles	4.00	4.04	Seoul	20.30	20.30
Lourenço Marques	14.00	14.12	Shanghai	20.00	20.5
Madeira	11.00	10.55	Singapore	19.30	18.55
Madras	17.30	17.21	Smyrna	14.00	13.49
Madrid	13.00	11.45	Stockholm	13.00	13.12
Malta	13.00	12.58	Suez	14.00	14.11
Manila (Philippine			Sydney	22.00	22.5
Is.)	20.00	20.3	Tangier	12.00	11.36
Mecca	14.40	14.40	Tokyo	21.00	21.20
Melbourne	22.00	21.40	Toronto	7.00	6.42
Mexico City	6.00	5.25	Tripoli	13.00	12.53
Montevideo	9.00	8.15	Vancouver	4.00	3.55
Montreal	7.00	7.6	Vienna	13.00	13.5
Moscow	15.00	14.30	Wellington	24.00	23.38
New Orleans	6.00	6.1	Winnipeg	6.00	5.32
New York	7.00	7.4			

Where Summer Time applies through part of the year only (see page 45 local clock time is usually one hour ahead of that shown.

Foreign Money

In the table on page 48 are shown foreign monetary units (the monetary unit of the UK is the £ sterling).

The values of foreign money in relation to that of the UK change somewhat from time to time. A bank will always give the exact day-to-day value of any particular foreign money if asked.

Country	Monetary Unit	Country	Monetary Unit
Argentina	Argentinian Peso	Italy	Lira
Australia	Australian $	Japan	Yen
Austria	Schilling	Lebanon	Lebanese £
Belgium	Belgian Franc	Luxembourg	Luxembourg Franc
Bolivia	Bolivian Peso		
Brazil	New Cruzeiro	Malaysia	Malaysian $
Bulgaria	Lev	Mexico	Mexican Peso
Burma	Kyat	Netherlands	Guilder
Canada	Canadian $	New Zealand	New Zealand $
Ceylon	Ceylon Rupee	Nicaragua	Cordoba
Chile	Chilean Escudo	Norway	Norwegian Krone
China	People's $		
Colombia	Columbian Peso	Pakistan	Pakistan Rupee
Costa Rica	Colon	Panama	Balboa
Cuba	Cuban Peso	Paraguay	Guarani
Czechoslovakia	Koruna	Peru	Sol
Denmark	Danish Krone	Philippines	Phillippine Peso
Dominican		Poland	Zloty
Republic	Dominican Peso	Portugal	Portuguese Escudo
Ecuador	Sucre		
Finland	Markka	Rumania	Lev
France	Franc	Salvador	Colon
Germany		South Africa	Rand
(East)	Ostmark	Spain	Peseta
(West)	Deutschemark	Sweden	Swedish Kronor
Greece	Drachma	Switzerland	Swiss Franc
Guatemala	Quetzal	Thailand	Baht
Haiti	Gourde	Turkey	Turkish £
Honduras	Lempira	United Arab	
Hong Kong	HK $	Republic	Egyptian £
Iceland	Icelandic Krona	United States	US $
India	Indian Rupee	USSR	Rouble
Indonesia	Rupiah	Uruguay	Uruguayan Peso
Iran	Rial	Venezuela	Bolivar
Iraq	Iraqi Dinar	Yugoslavia	New Dinar
Israel	Israeli £		

Further Reading

Pictorial History of the Ancient World, Ella Anderson (Odhams).
Hamlyn's New Relief World Atlas, Ed. Shirley Carpenter (Paul Hamlyn).
Collins' Pocket Atlas of the World (Collins).
Standard Encyclopedia of the World's Oceans and Islands, Ed. Anthony
  Huxley (Weidenfeld & Nicolson).
Children's Encyclopedia of Knowledge, Book of Our World (Collins).
The Boys' Book of Engineering Wonders, Leonard Bertin (Burke).

Science and Mathematics

Experiment is the key to our knowledge of the world around us, what
it is made of and how various materials behave. Scientists have found
out all that they know about the composition and behaviour of materials
by carrying out experiments, working out theories and then putting their
theories to the test in more experiments.

For many of us the chance of carrying out experiments – whether
they are going to produce gases that stink or merely to find out the
density of a lump of metal by weighing it and measuring its volume –
is the feature which attracts us most of all to studying science.

Unfortunately, there is not enough space here to give details of any
experiments, but that is not the purpose of the book. Rather it sets out
to give lists and tables of facts with just sufficient explanation to give
the facts some meaning. However, the lists of books for further reading
at the end of the chapter includes some which give details of experiments.

Inventions and Discoveries

Achievement	Date	Inventor/Discoverer
Adding Machine	1642	Blaise Pascal (French)
Arc Lamp	1879	C. F. Brush (US)
Aspirin	1893	Hermann Dreser
Bakelite	1907	Leo H. Baekeland (Belgian/US)
Barometer	1643	Evangelista Torricelli (Italian)
Bifocal lens	1780	Benjamin Franklin (US)
Bunsen burner	1855	Robert von Bunsen (German)
Carbon dioxide and gases generally	1848	Johann Baptista van Helmont (Belgian)

Achievement	Date	Inventor/Discoverer
Celluloid	1861	Alexander Parkes (British)
Cement (Portland)	1824	Joseph Aspdin (British)
Chronometer	1735	John Harrison (British)
Clock (mechanical)	725	I-Hsing and Liang Ling-Tsan (Chinese)
Clock (pendulum)	1657	Christian Huygens (Dutch)
Combustion (Theory of)	1775	Antoine Lavoisier (French)
DDT	1939	Paul Müller (Swiss)
Dyes (synthetic)	1857	William Perkins (British)
Dynamo	1860	Antonio Picinotti (Italian)
Electric generator (static)	1660	Otto von Guericke (German)
Electric lamp	1879	Thomas Edison (US)
Electric motor (d.c.)	1873	Zénobe Gramme (Belgium)
(a.c.)	1888	Nikola Tesla (US)
Electro magnet	1824	William Sturgeon (British)
Electrometer	1788	Alessandro Volta (Italian)
Electronic computer	1942	J. G. Brainerd, J. P. Eckert, J. W. Manchly (USA)
Fluorine	1771	Wilhelm Scheele (Swedish)
Gravity	1682	Isaac Newton (British)
Gyro compass	1911	Elmer Sperry (US)
Hydrogen	1766	Henry Cavendish (British)
Laser	1960	Charles Towney (US)
Light (Wave theory of)	1690	Christian Huygens (Dutch)
Logarithms	1614	John Napier (Scots)
Magnetism	1600	William Gilbert (English)
Margarine	1863	Hippolyte Mège-Mouries (French)
Microphone	1876	Alexander Graham Bell (US)
Microscope (optical)	1590	Zacharias Jansen (Dutch)
Microscope (electron)	1939	Vladimir Zworykin (Russian/US)
Morphine	1805	Friedrich Sertürner (German)
Nitrogen	1772	Daniel Rutherford (British)
Nylon	1937	Wallace Carothers (US)
Oxygen	1774	Joseph Priestley (British) Wilhelm Scheele (Swedish)
Pendulum	1602	Galileo Galilei (Italian)
Photography (on metal)	1826	J. Nicéphore Niépce (French)
Penicillin	1940	Alexander Fleming (British)
Radar	1935	Robert Watson-Watt (British)
Radio telegraphy	1895	Lord Rutherford (New Zealander)
Radium	1898	Pierre and Marie Curie (French)
Rare gases	1894–8	William Ramsey (British)

Achievement	Date	Inventor/Discoverer
Rayon	1883	Joseph Swan (British)
Rubber (latex foam)	1928	E. A. Murphy (British)
Rubber (vulcanized)	1841	Charles Goodyear (US)
Silicones	1904	F. S. Kipping (British)
Slide rule	1621	William Oughtred (British)
Sodium	1807	Humphry Davy (British)
Steel production	1855	Henry Bessemer (British)
Telegraph	1837	William Coke, Charles Wheatstone (British)
Telephone	1861	J. Philip Reis (German)
Telescope	1608	Hans Lippershey (Dutch)
Television	1926	John Logie Baird (British)
Terylene	1941	J. R. Whinfield, J. T. Dickson (British)
Thermometer	1593	Galileo Galilei (Italian)
Transistor	1948	Walter Brittain (US)
Vitamins	1930	Frederick Hopkins (British)
X-rays	1895	Wilhelm von Röntgen (German)

Basic Laws of Physics and Chemistry

Archimedes' Principle. Floating objects and objects which are completely submerged in a liquid experience an upthrust equal to the weight of liquid displaced by the object.

Avogardo's Law. Equal volumes of all gases under the same conditions of temperature and pressure contain the same number of molecules.

Boyle's Law. The volume of a given quantity (mass) of any gas varies inversely as the pressure acting upon it, provided that the temperature of the gas remains unchanged.

Charles' Law. The volume occupied by a given quantity (mass) of gas is directly proportional to its absolute temperature, provided that the pressure of the gas remains unchanged.

Law of Constant Composition. A definite chemical compound always contains the same elements chemically combined in the same proportions by weight.

Law of Conservation of Mass. In all ordinary chemical reactions the total mass of the reactants is always equal to the total mass of the products, which is another way of saying that matter can neither be created nor destroyed.

Law of Conservation of Energy. Except in thermonuclear reactions, energy can neither be created nor destroyed; it is merely transformed from one form to another.

Faraday's Laws of Electrolysis. (1) The weight of an ion formed or deposited at an electrode is proportional to the quantity of electricity (number of coulombs) which is passed through the electrolyte. (2) The weights of ions formed or deposited by the same quantity of electricity are in the ratio of their chemical equivalents.

The Gas Law. Changes in the volume (V) of a gas as its pressure (P) and absolute temperature (T) are varied may be predicted by the equation $PV = RT$, where R is a constant. This relationship, which is not followed exactly under extremes of temperature or pressure is a combination of Boyle's and Charles' laws.

Graham's Law of Diffusion. The relative rates of diffusion of different gases under identical conditions are inversely proportional to the square roots of their densities.

Hooke's Law. Provided the elastic limit is not exceeded, the extension of an elastic spring is proportional to the force producing the extension.

Law of Multiple Proportions. When two elements combine to form more than one compound, the weights of the first element which combine separately with a fixed weight of the second are in the ratio of whole numbers, usually small.

Newton's Laws of Motion.
(1) Every body continues in a state of rest or of uniform motion in a straight line unless it is compelled by an external force to change that state.

(2) Rate of change of momentum is proportional to the applied force and takes place in the direction in which the force acts.

(3) To every action there is an equal and opposite reaction.

Ohm's Law. Providing its physical conditions (*e.g.* its temperature) do not alter, the current flowing through a wire is directly proportional to the potential difference between the ends of the wire.

Theorem of Parallelogram of Forces. If two forces acting at a point are represented in size and direction by the two sides of a parallelogram drawn from a point, the resultant of the two forces is represented in size and direction by the diagonal of the parallelogram drawn from that point.

Law of Reciprocal Proportions. Elements combine with one another to form compounds in the ratio of their chemical equivalents, or in some simple multiple or sub-multiple of that ratio.

Laws of Reflection.
(1) The incident ray, the reflected ray and the normal to the reflecting surface at the point of incidence lie in the same plane.

(2) The angle between the incident ray and the normal (*i.e.* the angle of incidence) is equal to the angle between the reflected ray and the normal.

Snell's Laws of Refraction.
(1) The incident ray, the refracted ray and the normal to the surface separating the two media at the point of incidence lie in the same plane.

(2) The ratio of the sine of the angle of incidence to the sine of the angle of refraction is a constant for any pair of media.

Laws of Thermodynamics.
(0) If two objects are in thermal equilibrium with a third object, then they are in thermal equilibrium with each other.

(1) Heat and mechanical work are mutually convertible, and in any operation involving such a conversion one calorie of heat is equivalent to $4\cdot18 \times 10^{-7}$ ergs of mechanical work.

(2) Heat cannot be transferred from a colder to a hotter body by a continuous, self-sustaining process, *i.e.* heat cannot flow 'uphill' of its own accord.

(3) It is impossible to cool matter down to the absolute zero of temperature.

Table of Elements

Over 100 chemical elements have now been identified by scientists. Of these, 88 are known to occur in nature either by themselves or in combination with other elements. The remainder have been produced artificially, either as a result of radio-active decay or through nuclear bombardment. The table lists the chemical symbol, atomic number and atomic weight of all known elements.

Element	Symbol	At. No.	At. Wt.	Element	Symbol	At. No.	At. Wt.
Actinium	Ac	89	[227]	Gadolinium	Gd	64	157·3
Aluminium	Al	13	27·0	Gallium	Ga	31	69·7
Americium	Am	95	[243]	Germanium	Ge	32	72·6
Antimony	Sb	51	121·8	Gold	Au	79	197·0
Argon	Ar	18	39·9	Hafnium	Hf	72	178·5
Arsenic	As	33	74·9	Helium	He	2	4·0
Astatine	At	85	[210]	Holmium	Ho	67	164·9
Barium	Ba	56	137·3	Hydrogen	H	1	1·0
Berkelium	Bk	97	[249]	Indium	In	49	114·8
Beryllium	Be	4	9·0	Iodine	I	53	126·9
Bismuth	Bi	83	209·0	Iridium	Ir	77	192·2
Boron	B	5	10·8	Iron	Fe	26	55·8
Bromine	Br	35	79·9	Krypton	Kr	36	83·8
Cadmium	Cd	48	112·4	Kurchatovium	Ku	104	[260]
Caesium	Cs	55	132·9	Lanthanum	La	57	138·9
Calcium	Ca	20	40·1	Lawrencium	Lw	103	[257]
Californium	Cf	98	[249]	Lead	Pb	82	207·2
Carbon	C	6	12·0	Lithium	Li	3	6·9
Cerium	Ce	58	140·1	Lutetium	Lu	71	175·0
Chlorine	Cl	17	35·5	Magnesium	Mg	12	24·3
Chromium	Cr	24	52·0	Manganese	Mn	25	54·9
Cobalt	Co	27	58·9	Mendelevium	Md	101	[256]
Copper	Cu	29	63·5	Mercury	Hg	80	200·6
Curium	Cm	96	[247]	Molybdenum	Mo	42	95·9
Dysprosium	Dy	66	162·5	Neodymium	Nd	60	144·2
Einsteinium	Es	99	[254]	Neon	Ne	10	20·2
Erbium	Er	68	167·3	Neptunium	Np	93	[237]
Europium	Eu	63	152·0	Nickel	Ni	28	58·7
Fermium	Fm	100	[253]	Niobium	Nb	41	92·9
Fluorine	F	9	19·0	Nitrogen	N	7	14·0
Francium	Fr	87	[223]	Nobelium	No	102	[254]

Element	Symbol	At. No	At. Wt.	Element	Symbol	At. No.	At. Wt.
Osmium	Os	76	190·2	Silver	Ag	47	107·9
Oxygen	O	8	16·0	Sodium	Na	11	23·0
Palladium	Pd	46	106·4	Strontium	Sr	38	87·6
Phosphorus	P	15	31·0	Sulphur	S	16	32·1
Platinum	Pt	78	195·1	Tantalum	Ta	73	180·9
Plutonium	Pu	94	[244]	Technetium	Tc	43	[99]
Polonium	Po	84	[209]	Tellurium	Te	52	127·6
Potassium	K	19	39·1	Terbium	Tb	65	158·9
Praseodymium	Pr	59	140·9	Thallium	Tl	81	204·4
Promethium	Pm	61	[147]	Thorium	Th	90	[232]
Protactinium	Pa	91	[231]	Thulium	Tm	69	168·9
Radium	Ra	88	[226]	Tin	Sn	50	118·7
Radon	Rn	86	[222]	Titanium	Ti	22	47·9
Rhenium	Re	75	186·2	Tungsten	W	74	183·9
Rhodium	Rh	45	102·9	Uranium	U	92	[238]
Rubidium	Rb	37	85·5	Vanadium	V	23	50·9
Ruthenium	Ru	44	101·1	Xenon	Xe	54	131·3
Samarium	Sm	62	105·4	Ytterbium	Yb	70	173·0
Scandium	Sc	21	45·0	Yttrium	Y	39	88·9
Selenium	Se	34	79·0	Zinc	Zn	30	65·4
Silicon	Si	14	28·1	Zirconium	Zr	40	91·2

The atomic weights [in brackets] of the radio-active elements are those of the most stable isotopes of the elements concerned. Actinium, polonium, protactinium, radium, radon, thorium and uranium occur in nature, but all other radio-active elements have so far only been obtained artificially.

Chemical Formulae

Acetaldehyde: CH_3CHO
Acetic acid: CH_3COOH
Acetone: CH_3COCH_3
Acetylene: C_2H_2
Alcohol (Ethyl): CH_3CH_2OH
Aluminium chloride: $AlCl_3$
Aluminium hydroxide: $Al(OH)_3$
Aluminium oxide: Al_2O_3
Aluminium sulphate: $Al_2(SO_4)_3$
Ammonia: NH_3

Ammonium carbonate:
$(NH_4)_2CO_3$
Ammonium chloride: NH_4Cl
Ammonium nitrate: NH_4NO_3
Ammonium sulphate: $(NH_4)_2SO_4$
Amyl acetate: $CH_3COOC_5H_{11}$
Aniline: $C_6H_5NH_2$
Barium chloride: $BaCl_2$
Barium hydroxide: $Ba(OH)_2$
Barium sulphate: $BaSO_4$

Benzaldehyde: C_6H_5CHO
Benzene: C_6H_6
Borax: $Na_2B_4O_7$
Boric acid: H_3BO_3
Bromoform: $CHBr_3$
Calcium bromide: $CaBr_2$
Calcium carbide: CaC_2
Calcium carbonate: $CaCO_3$
Calcium chloride: $CaCl_2$
Calcium hydroxide: $Ca(OH)_2$
Calcium oxide: CaO
Calcium sulphate: $CaSO_4$
Calcium sulphide: CaS
Carbon dioxide: CO_2
Carbon monoxide: CO
Carbon tetrachloride: CCl_4
Chloroform: $CHCl_3$
Chrome alum:
  $K_2SO_4.Cr_2(SO_4)_3.24H_2O$
Chromium oxide: Cr_2O_3
Copper nitrate: $Cu(NO_3)_2$
Copper oxide (Cupric): CuO
Copper oxide (Cuprous): Cu_2O
Copper sulphate: $CuSO_4$
Copper sulphide: CuS
Dextrose: $C_6H_{12}O_6$
Ether (Ethyl): $(C_2H_5)_2O$
Ethyl alcohol: CH_3CH_2OH
Ethylene: C_2H_4
Ethyl chloride: C_2H_5Cl
Ferrous ammonium sulphate:
  $(NH_4)_2SO_4,FeSO_4,6H_2O$
Ferric chloride: $FeCl_3$
Ferric hydroxide: $Fe(OH)_3$
Ferric oxide: Fe_2O_3
Ferrous carbonate: $FeCO_3$
Ferrous oxide: FeO
Ferrous sulphate: $FeSO_4$
Formaldehyde: $HCHO$
Formic acid: $HCOOH$
Glycerin: $CH_2OH \cdot CHOH \cdot CH_2OH$
Hydrochloric acid: HCl

Hydrogen peroxide: H_2O_2
Hydrogen sulphide: H_2S
Iodoform: CHI_3
Lactose: $C_{12}H_{22}O_{11}$
Lead acetate: $(CH_3COO)_2Pb$
Lead carbonate (basic):
  $2PbCO_3,Pb(OH)_2$
Lead monoxide (Litharge): PbO
Lead oxide (Red lead): Pb_3O_4
Lead sulphate: $PbSO_4$
Lead sulphide: PbS
Magnesium chloride: $MgCl_2$
Magnesium hydroxide: $Mg(OH)_2$
Magnesium oxide: MgO
Magnesium peroxide: MgO_2
Magnesium phosphate: $Mg_3(PO_4)_2$
Magnesium sulphate: $MgSO_4$
Manganese dioxide: MnO_2
Mercuric oxide: HgO
Mercuric sulphate: $HgSO_4$
Mercurous sulphate: Hg_2SO_4
Methane: CH_4
Methyl alcohol: CH_3OH
Methyl chloride: CH_3Cl
Methyl iodide: CH_3I
Naphthalene: $C_{10}H_8$
Nickel oxide: NiO
Nitric acid: HNO_3
Nitric oxide: NO
Nitrobenzene: $C_6H_5NO_2$
Nitrous acid: HNO_2
Nitrous oxide: N_2O
Oxalic acid: $(COOH)_2$
Phenol: C_6H_5OH
Phenolphthalein: $C_{22}H_{14}O_4$
Phosphoric acid: H_3PO_4
Phosphorous acid: HPO_3
Potassium aluminium sulphate
  (alum): $K_2SO_4,Al_2(SO_4)_3,24H_2O$
Potassium bicarbonate: $KHCO_3$
Potassium bichromate: $K_2Cr_2O_7$
Potassium bromide: KBr

Potassium carbonate: K_2CO_3
Potassium chlorate: $KClO_3$
Potassium chloride: KCl
Potassium chromate: K_2CrO_4
Potassium iodide: KI
Potassium manganate: K_2MnO_4
Potassium nitrate: KNO_3
Potassium nitrite: KNO_2
Potassium permanganate: $KMnO_4$
Potassium sulphate: K_2SO_4
Potassium sulphide: K_2S
Propylene: C_3H_6
Quinol: $C_6H_4(OH)_2$
Saccharin: $C_6H_4CO\cdot SO_2NH$
Sodium bicarbonate: $NaHCO_3$
Sodium bromide: $NaBr$
Sodium carbonate: Na_2CO_3
Sodium chlorate: $NaClO_3$
Sodium chloride: $NaCl$

Sodium hydroxide: $NaOH$
Sodium nitrate: $NaNO_3$
Sodium nitrite: $NaNO_2$
Sodium phosphate: Na_2HPO_4
Sodium sulphate: Na_2SO_4
Sodium sulphite: Na_2SO_3
Sodium thiosulphate: $Na_2S_2O_3$
Sulphuric acid: H_2SO_4
Sulphurous acid: H_2SO_3
Stannic oxide: SnO_2
Strontium carbonate: $SrCO_3$
Strontium chloride: $SrCl_2$
Strontium nitrate: $Sr(NO_3)_2$
Sucrose: $C_{12}H_{22}O_{11}$
Sulphur dioxide: SO_2
Sulphur trioxide: SO_3
Water: H_2O
Zinc chloride: $ZnCl_2$
Zinc oxide: ZnO
Zinc sulphate: $ZnSO_4$

Chemical and Common Names of Familiar Substances

Accumulator acid	Moderately strong sulphuric acid (H_2SO_4) containing about 34 per cent concentrated acid and 66 per cent distilled water. The specific gravity of the solution should be about 1·25.
Alum	Potassium aluminium sulphate [$K_2SO_4, Al_2(SO_4)_3, 24H_2O$].
Aqua fortis	Concentrated nitric acid (HNO_3).
Aqua regia	Mixture of concentrated nitric and hydrochloric acids in ratio of 1 part HNO_3 to 4 parts HCl.
Blue vitriol	Crystalline copper sulphate ($CuSO_4, 5H_2O$).
Boracic acid	Boric acid (H_3BO_3).
Borax	Sodium pyroborate ($Na_2B_4O_7$).
Bromide	Potassium bromide (KBr).
Carbolic acid	Phenol (C_6H_5OH).
Carbonic acid gas	Carbon dioxide (CO_2)
Caustic soda	Sodium hydroxide ($NaOH$).
Chalk	Calcium carbonate ($CaCO_3$).
Common salt	Sodium chloride ($NaCl$).
Epsom salt	Crystalline magnesium sulphate ($MgSO_4, 7H_2O$).

Firedamp	Methane (CH_4).
Glauber's salt	Crystalline sodium sulphate ($Na_2SO_4, 10H_2O$).
Green vitriol	Crystalline ferrous sulphate ($FeSO_4, 7H_2O$).
Hypo	Sodium thiosulphate ($Na_2S_2O_3$).
Lime	Calcium oxide (CaO).
Magnesia	Magnesium oxide (MgO).
Muriate of potash	Potassium chloride (KCl).
Natural gas	Mixture of inflammable gases which issues from holes in the Earth's crust in certain localities. Methane (CH_4) is usually the main constituent.
Nitre	Potassium nitrate (KNO_3).
Oil of vitriol	Concentrated sulphuric acid (H_2SO_4).
Plaster of Paris	Form of calcium sulphate having the formula $CaSO_4, \frac{1}{2}H_2O$.
Quicklime	Calcium oxide (CaO).
Potash	Potassium carbonate (K_2CO_3).
Red lead	Red lead oxide (Pb_3O_4).
Sal ammoniac	Ammonium chloride (NH_4Cl).
Saltpetre	Potassium nitrate (KNO_3).
Sal volatile	Ammonium carbonate $[(NH_4)_2CO_3]$.
Salts of lemon	Potassium hydrogen oxalate $[KH_3(OOC)_4, 2H_2O]$.
Slaked lime	Calcium hydroxide $[Ca(OH)_2]$.
Spirits of salt	Solution of hydrochloric acid (HCl).
Vinegar	Solution of acetic acid (CH_3COOH).
Washing soda	Crystalline sodium carbonate ($Na_2CO_3, 10H_2O$).

Useful Formulae in Physics

Mechanics
Equations of Motion

$$v = u + at \qquad s = \frac{u + v}{2} t$$

$$s = ut + \tfrac{1}{2}at^2 \qquad v^2 = u^2 + 2as$$

where a = acceleration u = initial velocity
v = final velocity s = distance
t = time

Pendulum

$$t = 2\pi \sqrt{\frac{l}{g}}$$

where t = time of one complete swing (once in each direction)
l = length of pendulum
g = acceleration due to gravity

Machines

mechanical advantage $= \dfrac{\text{load}}{\text{effort}}$

velocity ratio $= \dfrac{\text{distance moved by effort}}{\text{distance moved by load}}$

efficiency $= \dfrac{\text{work done by machine}}{\text{energy put into machine}} = \dfrac{\text{mechanical advantage}}{\text{velocity ratio}}$

Mirrors and Lenses

$$\frac{1}{u} + \frac{1}{v} = \frac{1}{f}$$

where u = distance of object from mirror or lens
v = distance of image from mirror or lens
f = focal length of mirror or lens (for convex mirrors and concave lenses f is negative).
(Distances from mirror/lens to real objects/images are positive and to virtual objects/images negative.)

In all the above formulae the value of one remaining unknown can be found by substituting appropriate value of all the other quantities. **Always take care to use the same units throughout:** *for instance, do not mix times in minutes with speeds in miles per hour in the equations of motion (it is usually best to convert times to seconds).*

Electricity

Ohm's Law

$$E = IR \qquad R = \frac{E}{I} \qquad I = \frac{E}{R} \qquad W = IE = I^2 R = \frac{E^2}{R}$$

where E = potential difference (in volts), I = current (in amperes), R = resistance (in ohms), and W = power (in watts).

Resistances

$$\text{in series, } R = R_1 + R_2 + R_3, \text{ etc.}$$

$$\text{in parallel, } \frac{1}{R} = \frac{1}{R_1} + \frac{1}{R_2} + \frac{1}{R_3}, \text{ etc.}$$

where R = resistance (in ohms).

Capacitors

$$\text{in series, } \frac{1}{C} = \frac{1}{C_1} + \frac{1}{C_2} + \frac{1}{C_3}, \text{ etc.}$$

$$\text{in parallel, } C = C_1 + C_2 + C_3, \text{ etc.}$$

where C = capacity (in farads or in microfarads).

Frequency and Wavelength

$$n = \frac{300,000}{\lambda}, \text{ and } \lambda = \frac{300,000}{n}$$

where n = frequency (in kiloHertz) and λ = wavelength (in metres).

Plane and Solid Figures (Figs 1 and 2)

Triangle: Any plane figure enclosed by three straight lines. (A)
Right-angled triangle: A triangle containing one right angle. (B)
Isosceles triangle: A triangle having two sides of equal length. (C)
Equilateral triangle: A triangle having all three sides of equal length. (D)
  The area of a triangle is half of the length of its base multiplied by its perpendicular height ($\frac{1}{2} b \times h$). (A)

Quadrilateral: Any plane figure enclosed by four straight lines. (E)
Trapezium: A quadrilateral having one pair of sides parallel. (F)
Parallelogram: A quadrilateral having both pairs of opposite sides parallel. (G)
Rhombus: A quadrilateral having all sides equal in length. (H)
Square: A quadrilateral having all sides equal in length and all angles equal (*i.e.* all right angles). (I)
Rectangle: A quadrilateral with all angles equal (*i.e.* all right angles). (J)
  The area of a trapezium is half the sum of the lengths of its parallel sides multiplied by the perpendicular distance between them [$\frac{1}{2} (a + b) \times c$]. (F)
  The area of a parallelogram is length of one side multiplied by the perpendicular distance to the opposite side ($d \times e$). (G)

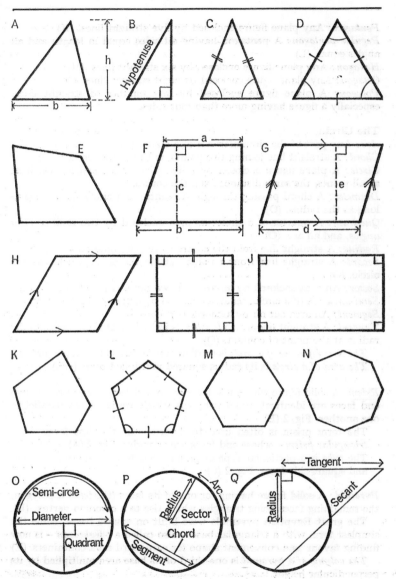

Fig. 1. Plane figures.

Pentagon: Any plane figure enclosed by five straight lines. (K)

Regular pentagon: A pentagon having all sides equal in length and all angles equal. (L)

Hexagon: Any plane figure enclosed by six straight lines. (M)

Octagon: Any plane figure enclosed by eight straight lines. (N)

Polygon: A plane figure enclosed by any number of straight lines, especially a figure having more than four sides.

The Circle

Arc: Any part of the circumference of a circle. (P)

Chord: A straight line joining two points on the circumference. (P)

Circle: A plane figure enclosed by a line (the circumference) which is, at all points, the same distance from the centre.

Diameter: A chord passing through the centre of a circle. It is twice as long as the radius. (O)

Quadrant: A quarter of a circle: an area enclosed by two radii at *right angles*, and an arc. (O)

Radius: A straight line from the centre to the circumference. (P)

Secant: A straight line from a point outside the circle which *cuts* the circle. (Q)

Sector: An area enclosed by an arc and two radii. (P)

Semi-circle: Half a circle: an area enclosed by an arc and a diameter. (O)

Segment: An area cut off by a chord. (P)

Tangent: A straight line which *touches* a circle. It is at right angles to the radius at the point of contact. (Q)

   The circumference of a circle is its diameter multiplied by π. (πd, or $2\pi r$.)
   The area of a circle is its radius squared multiplied by π. (πr^2.)

Prism: A solid figure whose side faces are parallelograms and whose two end faces are identical, equal polygons which are in planes parallel to one another. Fig. 2 (B)

   The term prism is often used to describe the simplest form – the *triangular prism* – whose end faces are triangles. Fig. 2 (A)

   The *cube* is a particular type of prism – one having square end faces and square side faces. Fig. 2 (C)

Pyramid: A solid figure having for one of its faces (the *base*) a polygon, the remaining faces being triangles which rise to a common vertex. (D)

   The great Egyptian pyramids were built on square bases, while the simplest form with a triangular base – also called a *tetrahedron* – is now finding favour as a convenient shape for cardboard milk containers. (E)

   The volume of a pyramid is one-third of its base area multiplied by its perpendicular height.

62

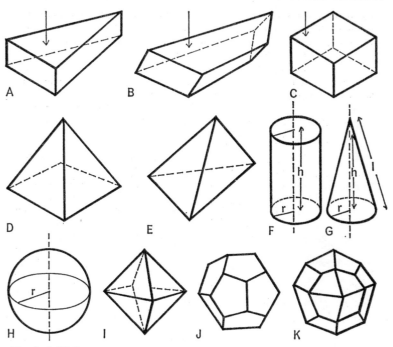

Fig. 2. Solid figures

Cone: A solid figure produced by rotating a line about an axis with which the line is not parallel. A cone is a pyramid on a circular base.(G)

> *Area of the curved surface of a cone* is half the circumference of its base (πr) multiplied by its slant height (l). ($\pi r l$.)
>
> *Volume of a cone* is one-third of its base area ($\frac{1}{3}\pi r^2$) multiplied by its perpendicular height (h). ($\frac{1}{3}\pi r^2 h$.)

Cylinder: A solid figure produced by rotating a line about a parallel axis. A cylinder is a prism having circular end faces. (F)

> *Area of the curved surface of a cylinder* is circumference of its base ($2\pi r$) multiplied by its height (h). ($2\pi r h$.)
>
> *Volume of a cylinder* is its base area (πr^2) multiplied by its height (h). ($\pi r^2 h$.)

Sphere: A solid figure produced by rotating a semi-circle about a diameter as axis. (H)

    Area of the surface of a sphere is $4\pi r^2$.

    Volume of a sphere is $\frac{4}{3}\pi r^3$.

Octahedron: A solid figure having eight faces, particularly one having eight triangular faces. (I)

Dodecahedron: A solid figure with twelve faces; the faces may be equal pentagons in a *regular dodecahedron*, or rhombs in a *rhombic dodecahedron*. (J & K)

Functions of π

$$\pi = 3{\cdot}14159 \left(or\ 3{\cdot}142\ or\ very\ approximately\ \frac{22}{7} \right)$$

$2\pi = 6{\cdot}2832$	$3\pi = 9{\cdot}4248$	$\frac{\pi}{2} = 1{\cdot}5708$
$\frac{\pi}{3} = 1{\cdot}0472$	$\frac{\pi}{4} = 0{\cdot}7854$	$\frac{4}{3}\pi = 4{\cdot}1888$
$\frac{1}{\pi} = 0{\cdot}3183$	$\frac{1}{2\pi} = 0{\cdot}1592$	$\log \pi = 0{\cdot}4971$

Trigonometrical Ratios

In a right-angled triangle

$$\sin A = \frac{\text{opposite}}{\text{hypoteneuse}} = \frac{a}{b}$$

$$\cos A = \frac{\text{adjacent}}{\text{hypoteneuse}} = \frac{c}{b}$$

$$\sec A = \frac{\text{hypoteneuse}}{\text{adjacent}} = \frac{b}{c}$$

$$\csc A = \frac{\text{hypoteneuse}}{\text{opposite}} = \frac{b}{a}$$

$$\tan A = \frac{\text{opposite}}{\text{adjacent}} = \frac{a}{c} \qquad \cot A = \frac{\text{adjacent}}{\text{opposite}} = \frac{c}{a}$$

Mathematical Signs

=	Is equal to	Σ	The sum of
≠	Is not equal to	δ	A small difference
≒	Is approx. equal to	$\angle$	Angle
≡	Is identical to	∞	Infinity
~	The difference between		
∝	Varies as		
>	Greater than	60 seconds (″) = 1 minute (′)
≯	Not greater than	60 minutes = 1 degree (°)
<	Less than	90 degrees = 1 right angle
≮	Not less than	4 right angles = 1 circle (360°)

English Weights and Measures

Length
    12 inches = 1 foot
    3 feet = 1 yard
    5½ yards = 1 pole
    22 yards (= 4 poles) = 1 chain
    220 yards (= 10 chains) = 1 furlong
    8 furlongs (= 1,760 yards) = 1 mile

Area
    144 sq. inches = 1 sq. foot
    9 sq. feet = 1 sq. yard
    30¼ sq. yards = 1 sq. rod, pole or perch
    40 sq. perches (= 1,210 sq. yards) = 1 rood
    4 roods (=4,840 sq. yards) = 1 acre
    640 acres = 1 sq. mile

Volume
    1,728 cubic inches = 1 cubic foot
    27 cubic feet = 1 cubic yard

Length at Sea
    6 feet = 1 fathom
    6,080 feet = 1 nautical mile
    (1 knot is a speed of 1 nautical mile/hour.)

c

Avoirdupois Weight
16 drams (*dr.*) = 1 ounce (*oz.*)
16 ounces = 1 pound (*lb.*)
7,000 grains = 1 pound
14 pounds = 1 stone
28 pounds = 1 quarter (*qr.*)
4 quarters (= 112 *lb.*) = 1 hundredweight (*cwt.*)
20 cwt (= 2,240 *lb.*) = 1 ton

Apothecaries' Weight (*Used for drugs*)
20 grains = 1 scruple (Ә)
3 scruples = 1 drachm (Ʒ)
8 drachms = 1 ounce (Ʒ)

Apothecaries' Liquid Measure (*Used for drugs*)
60 minims (m) or drops = 1 fluid drachm (*f*Ʒ)
8 fluid drachms = 1 fluid ounce (*f*Ʒ)
20 fluid ounces = 1 pint
(The Apothecaries' grain is the same as the Avoirdupois
grain, but the Apothecaries' oz. is the Troy oz.)

Troy Weight (*Used for precious metals*)
3·1683 grains (*gr.*) = 1 carat
24 grains = 1 pennyweight (*dwt.*)
20 pennyweights = 1 ounce
12 ounces = 1 pound (*lb.*)

Capacity
For Liquids and Solids
4 gills = 1 pint
2 pints = 1 quart
4 quarts = 1 (Imperial) gallon

For Solids only
2 gallons = 1 peck
4 pecks (= 8 gallons) = 1 bushel
8 bushels = 1 quarter

Metric Weights and Measures
(Only those metric units which are in regular use have been included in
the following list. However, all the prefixes (e.g. milli-, kilo-) used in form-
ing metric units are listed under 'Multiples and Sub-Multiples of
Numbers'. See page 70.)

Length
1,000 microns (μ) = 1 millimetre (*mm.*)
10 millimetres = 1 centimetre (*cm.*)
100 centimetres = 1 metre (*m.*)
1,000 metres = 1 kilometre (*km.*)

Area
100 sq. metres = 1 are
100 ares = 1 hectare
100 hectares = 1 sq. kilometre

Weight
1,000 milligrammes (*mg.*) = 1 gramme (*g.*)
1,000 grammes = 1 kilogramme (*kg.*)
1,000 kilogrammes = 1 tonne*

* Known as the *metric* ton (= 2,204 lb.) to avoid confusion with the *long* or *English* ton (= 2,240 lb.) and the *short* or *US* ton (= 2,000 lb.).

Capacity
1,000 millilitres (*ml.*) = 1 litre (*l.*)
1,000 litres = 1 kilolitre
1 kilolitre = 1 cubic metre

In May 1965 the President of the Board of Trade announced the intention of the UK to switch over to the metric system 'within ten years'. Many changes are likely in the period immediately following the introduction of decimal currency in February 1971. During the period of the changeover we shall have to use English and metric units side by side. Some products, notably pharmaceutical and toilet preparations ranging from ointments to shampoo, are already supplied in containers showing weight or capacity in metric units.

Conversion Tables – English
Length
1 inch	=	25·4 millimetres
1 foot	=	0·3048 metre
1 yard	=	0·9144 metre
1 fathom	=	1·8288 metres
1 pole	=	5·0292 metres
1 chain	=	20·117 metres
1 furlong	=	201·17 metres
1 mile	=	1·6093 kilometres

Area

1 sq. inch	=	6·4516 sq. centimetres
1 sq. foot	=	929·03 sq. centimetres
1 sq. yard	=	0·8361 sq. metre
1 sq. perch	=	25.293 sq. metres
1 rood	=	10·117 ares
1 acre	=	0·40469 hectare
1 sq. mile	=	259·00 hectares

Volume

1 cub. inch	=	16·387 cub. centimetres
1 cub. foot	=	0·028317 cub. metre
1 cub. yard	=	0·76455 cub. metre

Capacity

1 gill	=	142 millilitres
1 pint	=	568 millilitres
1 quart	=	1·136 litres
1 gallon	=	4·54596 litres
1 peck	=	9·092 litres
1 bushel	=	36·37 litres
1 quarter	=	0·29096 kilolitres

Avoirdupois

1 grain	=	0·0648 gram
1 dram	=	1·772 grams
1 ounce	=	28·350 grams
1 pound	=	0·45359 kilograms
1 stone	=	6·350 kilograms
1 quarter	=	12·70 kilograms
1 hundredweight	=	50·80 kilograms
1 (long) ton	=	1·016 metric tons

Apothecaries'

1 minim	=	0·059 millilitre
1 fluid scruple	=	1·184 millilitres
1 fluid drachm	=	3·552 millilitres
1 fluid ounce	=	28·4123 millilitres
1 pint	=	568 millilitres
1 grain	=	0·0648 gram
1 scruple (20 grains)	=	1·296 grams
1 drachm (3 scruples)	=	3·888 grams
1 oz. (8 drachms)	=	31·1035 grams

Troy

1 grain	=	0·0648 gram
1 pennyweight	=	1·5552 grams
1 troy ounce	=	31·1035 grams

Conversion Tables – Metric

Length

1 millimetre	=	0·03937 inch
1 centimetre	=	0·3937 inch
1 metre	=	$\begin{cases} 3\cdot28084 \text{ feet} \\ 1\cdot0936 \text{ yards} \end{cases}$
1 kilometre	=	0·62137 mile

Area

1 square centimetre	=	0·15500 sq. inch
1 square metre	=	$\begin{cases} 10\cdot7639 \text{ sq. feet} \\ 1\cdot1960 \text{ sq. yards} \end{cases}$
1 are	=	119·60 sq. yards
1 hectare	=	2·471 acres

Volume

1 cubic centimetre	=	0·061 cubic inch
1 cubic metre (1,000 cubic decimetres)	=	$\begin{cases} 35\cdot315 \text{ cubic feet} \\ 1\cdot30795 \text{ cubic yards} \end{cases}$

Capacity

1 litre	=	$\begin{cases} 1\cdot7598 \text{ pints} \\ 0\cdot220 \text{ gallons} \end{cases}$
1 kilolitre	=	27·5 bushels

Weight

Avoirdupois

1 milligram	=	0·15 grain
1 gram	=	$\begin{cases} 15\cdot432 \text{ grains} \\ 0\cdot03527 \text{ oz.} \end{cases}$
1 kilogram	=	2·2046 lb.
1 tonne	=	0·984 (long) ton

Troy

1 gram	=	$\begin{cases} 0\cdot03215 \text{ oz. troy} \\ 15\cdot432 \text{ grains} \end{cases}$

$$1 \text{ gram} = \begin{cases} \textit{Apothecaries'} \\ 0{\cdot}2572 \text{ drachm} \\ 0{\cdot}7716 \text{ scruple} \\ 15{\cdot}432 \text{ grains} \end{cases}$$

Multiples and Sub-multiples of Numbers

Metric System

The following is the full range (in ascending order of size) of prefixes used in forming metric units:

Prefix	Abbreviation	Multiplying factor
atto	a	0·000 000 000 000 000 001
femto	f	0·000 000 000 000 001
pico	p	0·000 000 000 001
nano	n	0·000 000 001
micro	μ	0·000 0001
milli	m	0·001
centi	c	0·01
deci	d	0·1
deca	da	10
hecto	h	100
kilo	k	1,000
mega	M	1,000,000
giga	G	1,000,000,000
terra	T	1,000,000,000,000

English System

dozen	12
score	20
hundred	5 score
great hundred	6 score (120)
gross	12 dozen (144)
great gross	12 gross (1728)

Miscellaneous

lakh (India)	= 100,000
crore (India)	= 100 lakh
	= 10,000,000
milliard	= 1,000,000,000
billion (USA and France)	= 1,000,000,000

| billion (UK) | = 1,000,000,000,000 |
| trillion (USA) | = 1,000,000,000,000 |

In view of the confusion over the value of a *billion* it is safer to talk of a *thousand million* or a *million million* (as the case may be) when it is not convenient to express the quantity in figures.

Rough Conversions

(Very approximate: intended for rough calculations only)

1 inch	=	$2\frac{1}{2}$ centimetres
1 foot	=	30 centimetres
1 acre	=	0·4 hectares
1 grain	=	65 milligrams
1 lb.	=	0·45 kilogram
7 quarts	=	8 litres
1 metre	=	$39\frac{1}{2}$ inches
1 kilometre	=	$\frac{5}{8}$ mile
1 kilogram	=	2·2 lb.
1 litre	=	$1\frac{3}{4}$ pints

Miscellaneous Measures

1 *gallon* of pure water weighs 10 lb.

A hand (when measuring a horse) is 4 inches.

A reputed quart (as in a bottle of wine, or spirit) is one-sixth of a gallon.

The gram (metric) is the weight of 1 cubic centimetre of pure water.

The litre (metric) is 1,000 cubic centimetres of pure water, and weighs 1 kilogram.

The British Thermal Unit (Btu) is the amount of heat required to raise 1 lb. of water by 1° F.

The Therm = 100,000 Btu.

The horsepower (H.P.) is the power needed to raise 550 lb. one foot in one second (or 33,000 lb. one foot in one minute).

The kilowatt (1,000 watts) is the power needed to raise 737·6 lb. one foot in one second (746 watts = 1 H.P.).

The Unit (Board of Trade unit, or B.o.T.U.) is consumption of electricity equal to 1,000 watts for one hour.

Temperature Scales

The Centigrade (or Celsius) temperature scale is used almost universally

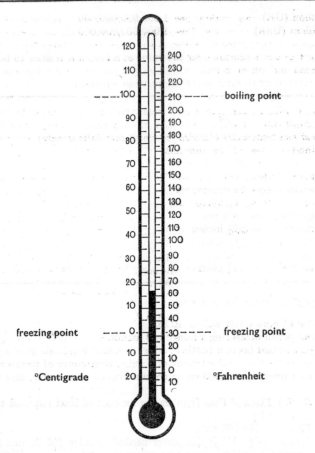

°Centigrade

°Fahrenheit

freezing point

boiling point

freezing point

Fig. 3. Fahrenheit and Celsius scales shown on the same thermometer

in scientific laboratories, while the other common scale – the Fahrenheit scale – is still used extensively in engineering both in the UK and USA. For many years weather reports in the UK gave temperatures in degrees Fahrenheit but in 1962 the Meteorological Office made the first step towards abandoning the Fahrenheit scale by giving the values of temperatures on both scales.

Until the Celsius scale is accepted universally, it will be necessary from time to time to convert temperatures from one scale to another. This is easily done by using simple arithmetic but various handy charts or tables can be used if great accuracy is not required and there are many temperatures to convert.

Temperature scales provide a means of comparing a particular temperature with certain reference points, the two most important being the temperature at which pure ice melts (often called the *lower fixed point*) and the temperature at which pure water boils under a pressure of one standard atmosphere (the *upper fixed point*).

On the Celsius scale the lower fixed point is designated 0° C., while the upper fixed point is 100° C. In contrast, the Fahrenheit scale ranges from 32° F. at the lower fixed point to 212° F. at the upper.

Thus 100 divisions or degrees between the two fixed points on the Celsius scale are equivalent to 180 divisions or degrees on the Fahrenheit scale. This reduces to the simpler ratio, 5 Celsius divisions are equivalent to 9 of the smaller Fahrenheit divisions. However, conversion between the two scales is complicated slightly because the two scales have different zeros.

To convert a Fahrenheit temperature to Celsius first subtract 32, then multiply by 5 and divide by 9. Thus to convert 98·4° F. (normal blood temperature).

$$98 \cdot 4 \text{ F}°. \equiv (98 \cdot 4 - 32) \text{ Fahrenheit degrees above ice point}$$
$$\equiv 66 \cdot 4 \text{ F}°. \text{ above ice point.}$$
$$180 \text{ F}°. \equiv 100 \text{ C}°.$$

$$1 \text{ F}°. \equiv \frac{100C}{180}°. = \frac{5C}{9}°.$$

$$66 \cdot 4 \text{ F}°. \text{ above ice point} \equiv \frac{5}{9} \times 66 \cdot 4 = 36 \cdot 9 \text{ C}°. \text{ above ice point}$$

$$= 36 \cdot 9 \text{ C}°.$$

Thus normal blood temperature is 36·9° C.

Conversely, to convert a Celsius temperature to Fahrenheit, first multiply by 9 and divide by 5, then finally add 32.

Every substance – even ice – contains a certain amount of heat. This is another way of saying that the molecules of any substance (the smallest possible part of the substance which can lead a separate existence) are constantly in motion: heating the substance gives the molecules more energy to move faster. The hotter the substance becomes the faster its molecules move. Conversely, cooling the substance slows down the molecules.

If we continue cooling the substance, the motion of the molecules eventually slows down so much that they stop moving altogether. The temperature at which this occurs (although no one has yet actually reached it) is the lowest that can be attained and is known as the *absolute zero*. On the Celsius scale absolute zero is $-273 \cdot 16°$ C., while on the Fahrenheit scale it is $-459 \cdot 69°$ F.

The Greek Alphabet

This alphabet is important because its letters are used so often in mathematical and scientific formulae and equations and to represent well-known constants such as the ratio of the circumference of a circle to its diameter (π). The word 'alphabet' itself is derived from the first two Greek letters.

Letter		Name	English Equivalent
A	α	Alpha	a
B	β	Beta	b
Γ	γ	Gamma	g (*hard*)
Δ	δ	Delta	d
E	ϵ	Epsilon	e (*short*)
Z	ζ	Zeta	z, dz
H	η	Eta	e (*long*)
Θ	θ	Theta	th
I	ι	Iota	i
K	κ	Kappa	k, *or hard* c
Λ	λ	Lambda	l
M	μ	Mu	m
N	ν	Nu	n
Ξ	ξ	Xi	x
O	o	Omicron	o (*short*)
Π	π	Pi	p
P	ρ	Rho	r
Σ	σ, s	Sigma	s
T	τ	Tau	t
Y	υ	Upsilon	u *or* y
Φ	ϕ	Phi	ph, f

Letter		Name	English Equivalent
X	χ	Chi	kh *or hard* ch
Ψ	ψ	Psi	ps
Ω	ω	Omega	o (*long*)

Further Reading

Men Who Changed the World; stories of invention and discovery, Egon Larsen (Phoenix).

Collins Children's Encyclopedia of Knowledge, Book of Science (Collins).

The Boys' Book of Modern Scientific Wonders, Leonard Bertin (Burke).

Understanding Science: a 12-volume encyclopedia originally published (1962–5) in 144 weekly parts (Sampson Low).

Science, Ed. by J. Bronowski (Macdonald).

Magnets, Bulbs and Batteries; *Light, Mirrors and Lenses*; *Air, Wind and Flight*; and *Levers, Pulleys and Engines*, F. E. Newing and Richard Bowood (Wills & Hepworth).

The Young Scientist's Approach to Light, T. H. Whitney (Warne).

The Young Scientist's Approach to Magnetism, T. H. Whitney (Warne).

The Magic of Electricity, Sam Rosenfeld (Faber).

How Much and How Many; the story of weights and measures, Jeanne Bendick (Brockhampton).

Exploring on Foot and Wheel

It is always enjoyable to hike through familiar countryside or to go exploring in new surroundings, but it can be far more exciting to have a definite objective on such expeditions. In fact to pursue a number of hobbies to the full, it is essential to go out into the countryside to gather information or collect specimens. You may already have such a hobby, but if you are looking for a new excuse to go exploring, why not try one of the following:

follow the course of a small river or stream to its source, starting each time from where you left off on the last hike;

make rubbings of the bark of various trees, or prints of their leaves and identify them;

visit a bird sanctuary, heronry or pond and count the number of birds seen;

see how many different types of stiles you can log and notice how many are made from materials that are available locally;

compare the way churches, and for that matter farm cottages, of different ages have been built;

go to the highest point in the neighbourhood with a map and compass to locate distant places and return on a finer (clearer) day to locate places even farther away;

find out about the history of villages by visiting their churches and other old buildings.

Planning the Route

Before setting out on an expedition – whether it is just for the afternoon or will occupy a whole week's holiday – it is well worth spending some time planning a route. In having a definite route – chosen to take in places where you are likely to see the things you are looking for – you will be able to make the best use of your time. This will also help you to get home at the time you were expected.

It is far better not to try to go too far at first – if you have time to spare you can always spend longer looking around an interesting village, or farm or searching in the woods for uncommon trees, or plants or for a badger's set.

A good map – 1 in. Ordnance Survey or ½ in. Bartholomew's – is essential both when planning the expedition and when you are out in the country-side. Other items which will come in useful include local guide books and bus and train time tables. Remember that some rural bus services are very infrequent and that some villages may only be served on the local market day.

It is far greater fun to go exploring with a few friends who have similar interests to your own. Furthermore, the companionship of the group will help you to pass the time if you are held up in a downpour, to cheer you up if you miss your way (though you should not do this if you have prepared yourselves by learning to read a map), or when you are tired at the end of a hot or hard day's walking and still have two miles to go to the nearest bus route or railway station. In such circumstances do not be tempted to accept lifts. You may get picked up by an undesirable person. Should you be delayed in your return, always try to telephone ahead to explain that you will be late in arriving.

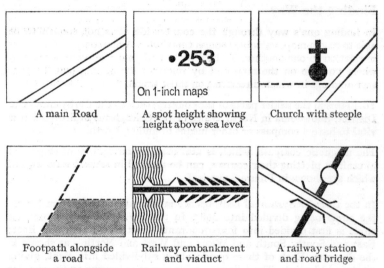

| A main Road | A spot height showing height above sea level | Church with steeple |
| Footpath alongside a road | Railway embankment and viaduct | A railway station and road bridge |

Fig. 4. Typical mapping symbols.

At first glance, a small-scale map of the type most useful for hiking appears very confusing since many objects of interest are identified only by symbols, but with a little practice one becomes familiar with maps and from then on they are constant and trusty companions on each and every expedition.

If maps are a mystery to you the first step in mastering their secrets is to learn the symbols used on them. A number of the more common ones are shown in Figure 4 but as different series of maps (and indeed different editions of the same series) sometimes use slightly different symbols, it is as well to study the key which is usually given at the foot of each sheet.

When you think you can recognize most of the symbols trace the route of a favourite walk on the map. All the time think of places which you pass and objects which you can see in the distance and compare these with what you can see on the map. When you have done this several times you can start to visualize from the map what you will find in reality.

Once you have become proficient you will find maps invaluable both out in the field and in planning your routes in advance.

Finding the Way

In finding one's way through the countryside, it is not enough to be able to read a map, valuable though this skill is. A map only shows places in relation to one another. To be able to find your way you must know where you are on the map and by referring to the map and to your surroundings in which direction you must travel.

To do this in the wilder parts of the country, such as the Derbyshire Peak District, Snowdonia in North Wales or the Cairngorms in Scotland it is vital to have a compass or other means of finding North.

The magnetic compass, which is also used by navigators of ships and aircraft in plotting their courses, can be marked in several ways two of which are shown in Figure 5 overleaf.

In the *Circular System* all bearings are measured clockwise from North, the circle being divided into 360°. In the *Point System* the compass circle is first divided into four quadrants – between North and East; East and South; South and West; and West and North – as shown in the diagram. Each of these quadrants is subdivided into eight, giving a total of 32 points. The following table gives the bearing on the circular system equivalent to each of the 32 points of the compass.

Points of the Compass	Circular	Points of the Compass	Circular
N.	0	S.E. by E.	$123\frac{3}{4}$
N. by E.	$11\frac{1}{4}$	S.E.	135
N.N.E.	$22\frac{1}{2}$	S.E. by S.	$146\frac{1}{4}$
N.E. by N.	$33\frac{3}{4}$	S.S.E.	$157\frac{1}{2}$
N.E.	45	S. by E.	$168\frac{3}{4}$
N.E. by E.	$56\frac{1}{4}$	S.	180
E.N.E.	$67\frac{1}{2}$	S. by W.	$191\frac{1}{4}$
E. by N.	$78\frac{3}{4}$	S.S.W.	$202\frac{1}{2}$
E.	90	S.W. by S.	$213\frac{3}{4}$
E. by S.	$101\frac{1}{4}$	S.W.	225
E.S.E.	$112\frac{1}{2}$	S.W. by W.	$236\frac{1}{4}$

Points of the Compass	Circular	Points of the Compass	Circular
W.S.W.	247½	N.W. by W.	303¾
W. by S.	258¾	N.W.	315
W.	270	N.W. by N.	326¼
W. by N.	281¼	N.N.W.	337½
W.N.W.	292½	N. by W.	348¾

But you can find North (or South) without a compass – provided that the sky is clear. In daytime you can use the Sun and a watch, and at night the stars. In the watch method you simply point the hour hand of the watch towards the Sun (after deducting one hour from 'Summer

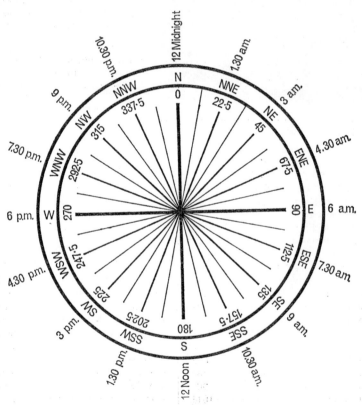

Fig. 5. A compass card marked in points and circular rotation.

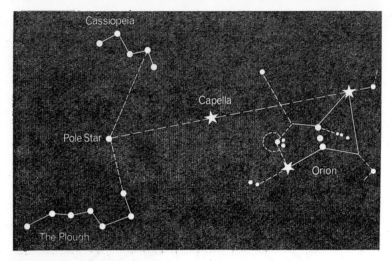

Fig. 6. Finding the north by the stars

Time' to get Sun time) and half-way between the hour hand and 12 on the dial is due South.

At night you can find North by locating the Pole Star (*Polaris*). This star is not very bright, but three constellations in the northern sky will lead you to it. Figure 6, which only shows the bright stars in the area concerned, indicates how you can find the position of the Pole Star once you have identified the Plough (*Ursa Major*), *Cassiopeia* or *Orion*.

Once you have found North you should turn your map around until the North pointer on the map points North, this is called *setting the map*. You will find on the map either two or three different North pointers – True or Geographic North (which is the North you find from the Sun or the North Star); Magnetic North (which is the direction shown by your compass, and which incidentally moves in the course of time) and possibly Grid North.

If you are quite certain where you are it is also possible to set the map by turning it until the position of landmarks shown on the map corresponds with the position of those objects in reality.

Being Prepared

One of the most important requirements for walking is to be suitably equipped with strong walking shoes – not high heels or plimsolls – and shorts or warm trousers depending upon the weather. As well as your map and compass you should always carry a wind- and water-proof anorak, spare warm clothing and emergency rations just in case you are delayed. You also need a small first aid kit in case of accidents.

Always leave behind you details of your route and *keep to it*, so that if you should not return at a reasonable hour your parents will know where to look for you.

Equipment for Hiking

The following lists will remind you of the items of equipment you will need to take with you on a hiking expedition. In each list items have been grouped together as an aid to gathering them before packing.

Personal Equipment (for expeditions)

Strong boots or shoes; plimsolls; anorak or other wind- and water-proof coat; thick sweater; spare clothing, including several pairs of thick socks; pyjamas or other change for the night.

Soap and towel; toothbrush and paste; brush and comb; metal mirror.

Map and compass; first aid kit; whistle; emergency rations; pocket knife; plastic water-bottle; money; post office savings book; rucksack.

Cooking Equipment

Cooking stove and fuel; matches; canteen or billycans.

Plastic bags and plastic containers (for keeping food in); tin and bottle opener; plate and mug; knife, fork and spoon.

Packing a rucksack is an art which can only be learned by experience. However, there are four rules which should be followed always. Pack items which you are going to need first at the top or in the side pockets, but keep the heaviest ones near the top as the rucksack is easier to carry that way. Also avoid putting hard pointed objects so that they dig into your back. At all costs avoid having anything hanging outside the rucksack.

An expedition can very easily be spoiled by having an overfull, heavy rucksack, so take care in selecting what you pack. You should aim to keep the weight of the rucksack and its contents below 25 lb. This can be achieved without much difficulty as many lightweight items are now available at reasonable cost. You should have no difficulty in keeping weight down as you can share such items as the cooking equipment with your companions.

Take particular care in selecting the foodstuffs which you carry with you. Avoid taking too many tinned foods as the tins are heavy. Many items of food, including milk, are now available in dehydrated form and as such are very light, though more expensive. Fresh meat is best bought on the day you are going to use it.

The Country Code

These ten simple rules were prepared by the National Parks Commission as a guide to those who do not fully understand the rural way of life, to guard against them doing harm to animals and farm machinery and to preserve the beauty of the countryside.

1   Guard against all risk of fire
2   Fasten all gates
3   Keep dogs under proper control
4   Keep to the paths across farm land
5   Avoid damaging fences, hedges and walls
6   Leave no litter
7   Safeguard water supplies
8   Protect wild life, wild plants and trees
9   Go carefully on country roads
10 Respect the life of the countryside

When cooking take particular care to observe Rules Nos. 1, 6 and 7. The risk of fire can be minimized by using a paraffin pressure stove or butane gas stove, rather than making a wood fire. But whichever you choose, take care in selecting the site for your fire. Keep away from hedges, haystacks or long grass – dry, barren ground is safest. If you choose a wood fire, always cut back turf from the fireplace which you can replace afterwards. Before you leave make absolutely certain that your fire is out by pouring water over the ground.

Always ask permission before cooking on private ground and if told you are trespassing, apologize and leave at once. To avoid contaminating the ground, streams, ponds and wells, whenever possible use public conveniences or ask permission of the owner of the land to use his W.C.

Nature Notes

The following are some of the wild flowers, trees and birds to look for on expeditions during different months of the year. Our native birds can be seen at all seasons, while many of the plants mentioned may flower later or possibly earlier depending upon the district and the weather.

January
Birds: Blackbird, black-headed gull, house sparrow, robin, rook, starling, thrush, tit.
Flowers: Common chickweed, furze or gorse, groundsel, shepherd's purse.
Trees: Catkins on hazel, alder.

February
Birds: Chaffinch, jackdaw, skylark, wood-pigeon, yellow-hammer. Many of our common birds begin nesting.
Flowers: Barren strawberry, lesser celandine.
Trees: Buds on the sallow (pussy willow) may be opening.

March
Birds: The migrants – chiffchaff, ring-ouzel, yellow wagtail, wheatear, willow warbler, wryneck and possibly sand-martin – are returning, while the fieldfare and redwing will be leaving for the north.
Flowers: Coltsfoot, daisy, ground ivy, marsh marigold, primrose, sweet violet, wood anemone.
Trees: Notice how the buds now beginning to appear show up clearly against the bare branches.

April
Birds: More of the summer migrants – blackcap, corncrake, cuckoo, house-martin, nightingale, swallow, swift, warblers, whitethroat – arrive.
Flowers: Arum (wake-robin, cuckoo-pint or lords and ladies), broom, dandelion, red dead-nettle, early purple orchid, greater stitchwort, speedwell, wood-sorrel.
Trees: Ash, beech, birch, oak, poplars, sallow are in bloom; also the almond and many fruit trees in orchards and gardens.

May
Birds: The last of the migrants – pied and spotted flycatcher, red-backed shrike – arrive.
Flowers: Bluebell, buttercup, cowslip, germander speedwell, Jack-by-the-hedge (garlic mustard), red and white clover, scarlet pimpernel, wild pansy.

Trees: Crab (or wild) apple, guelder rose, holly, hornbeam, hawthorn, horse-chestnut, laburnum, lilac, plane, rowan (mountain ash), Scots pine, spindle-tree, sycamore and wild cherry are in flower, as well as those mentioned under April.

June

Birds: Many fledglings (young birds) are to be seen this month. Their parents begin to moult.

Flowers: Common sorrel, common red poppy, cow parsnip (hogweed), dog rose, field bindweed (convolvulus), field scabious, foxglove, heartsease, meadowsweet, musk thistle, ox-eye daisy, ragged robin, ragwort, scentless mayweed, water crowfoot, yellow iris.

Trees: Lime and elder are in flower.

July

Birds: Some of the cuckoos leave.

Flowers: Bird's-foot trefoil (lady's slipper), cinquefoil, enchanter's nightshade, heather (ling), hedge parsley, honeysuckle, lady's bedstraw, rosebay willow-herb, silverweed, spear plume thistle.

Trees: Every tree is now in its full beauty; note particularly the elm, beech, birch and oak.

August

Birds: Blackcap, old cuckoos, nightingale and swift leave.

Flowers: Harebell (bluebell), nipplewort, stinging nettle, tansy.

Trees: Ash, horse-chestnut and sycamore begin to fruit. Close inspection under the leaves of other trees will reveal well-formed yet still small fruit.

September

Birds: Flycatchers, sand-martin, swallow, whitethroat and yellow wagtail all migrate to the south, while snipe arrive from the north.

Flowers: Marsh mallow, wild teazel and many of the flowers mentioned under July and August.

Trees: Beech, elder, hazel, horse-chestnut, holly, oak, plane, rowan, spindle-tree and yew are all fruiting.

October

Birds: The last of the migrants – house-martin and swallow – leave, but the winter migrants – fieldfare and redwing – arrive from Scandinavia.

Flowers: Autumn crocus.

Trees: The leaves have all changed colour and begin to fall. The ripe fruit of some trees adds further colour to the otherwise dull season.

November

Birds: Notice how the birds tend to fly about in flocks at this time of year.
Flowers: If the weather is not too severe you may find red clover, white campion, wild pansy and yarrow still in bloom.
Trees: Most of the trees are now bare, but the evergreens – fir, holly, laurel, Scots pine and yew – stand out clearly.

December

Birds: This is a good time for distinguishing our different native birds easily seen among the bare branches of the trees. Bitter weather will often send an unusual species to this country, so watch out for rare bird visitors.
Flowers: Flowers are few and far between in December, but many of those mentioned in the early months of the year can be found, also winter heliotrope and dwarf furze. However, the frost may well shrivel their flowers.
Trees: The holly, mistletoe and yew are berried and sometimes we can see tiny green catkins on the hazel. At this time of the year try to identify trees by their shape and bark patterns.

Using the Roads — Hints for Cyclists

If you want to explore a wider area than you can conveniently cover on foot and particularly if the places of interest which you want to see are far apart, you may find it convenient to use your cycle for exploring. This is healthier and cheaper than relying upon public transport to get you about and has the added advantage that you can travel at times which suit you.

But just as it is important to take care in the countryside, so too is it vital to observe the rules of the road. With the ever-increasing number of private cars and commercial vehicles on the roads, the cyclist must learn to tolerate them and above all to give very clear signals of what she is going to do so that other road users can act accordingly. Remember that because a bicycle is relatively unstable, and the cyclist has little protection, she is most likely to get injured irrespective of who is at fault, so take care!

The following general rules about cycling are taken from the *Highway Code* and have been drawn up for your guidance:

1. If a road has a special cycle track, always use it.

2. When cycling in company with others, never ride more than two abreast, so as to give other road users – especially fast motor traffic – plenty of room. If you are on a busy road, it is safest to ride in single file, keeping close to the left-hand kerb.

3. Never carry anything on your cycle which interferes with the handlebars or front wheel or brakes, or which is so awkward in shape or size that it makes balancing difficult.

4. Never hold on to another vehicle or another cyclist, and do not ride too close behind any other vehicle.

Apart from those rules, there are certain other things you must or must not do or you will be breaking the law. The most important of these are:

5. Always stop at traffic lights when they are against you, at pedestrian crossings when pedestrians are using them, and at 'Stop' and 'Give Way' signs. You must also stop when any policeman in uniform or traffic warden signals you to do so.

6. Unless you are riding a tandem cycle, you must never carry any other person on your cycle.

7. You must always have a red reflector showing to the rear of your cycle, and you must always show a red light to the rear and a white light to the front when riding during lighting-up time. If for any reason your lights will not work, you must walk your cycle, preferably along the pavement.

8. Your tyres must always be in good condition, and your brakes must always be efficient.

Road Signs and Signals

It is important when cycling to give other road-users very clear indications in advance of one's intentions. Figure 7 shows the hand signals which should be made by every cyclist.

If it is dangerous to take your hands off the handlebars to make any of these signals, pull into the side of the road and stop. Make sure there is no other traffic near by before going on.

Turning right   Turning left   Slowing down

Fig. 7. Cyclist's hand signals.

In addition, all road-users should know the meaning of road-signs. Some of the international, continental style of signs are shown in Figure 8.

The New Level Crossings

New level-crossing barriers, rather like those in use on the Continent, are being installed in many places. These barriers are worked automatically by approaching trains. Red flashing lights and a gong start to operate as a warning shortly before the barrier begins to fall. The barrier itself also has red lights on it.

Never pass any red lights when they are flashing or the gong when it is sounding, and never under any circumstances try to zig-zag past the barriers when they are down. You may think it is safe to do so because you have just seen a train pass; but as all the stop signs are still in operation another train is approaching – either in the opposite direction or following the first one.

Road Markings

When on any road which is marked with double white lines down the middle, the rules are:

If the line nearer to you is continuous, you must never cross it.

If the line nearer to you is broken, you may cross it for the purpose of overtaking; but you must be back on your correct side of the road before the start of any continuous line on that side.

These rules concern motorists more than cyclists; it is never safe for any cyclist on a busy road to be so far from the left-hand side of the road that she has to cross any line painted down the middle.

87

Warning Signs

Distance to stop sign ahead; Two-way traffic ahead; Steep hill downwards; Pedestrian crossing; Level crossing without gates or barrier; Traffic lights

Distance to give way sign ahead; Side road; Road works; Crossroads; Uneven Road; Roundabout

Orders

Give priority to vehicles from opposite direction; No waiting; Cycles prohibited; Cyclists only; Maximum speed limit; End of maximum speed limit

Stop and give way; Give way to traffic on major road; No entry; No right turn; No left turn; No U turns

Fig. 8. Road signs.

Pedestrian Crossings
The rules for crossing the road at 'zebra crossings' (which are indicated by flashing yellow lights) are:

88

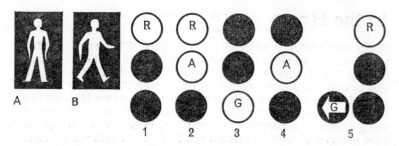

Fig. 9. Traffic signals. These must be obeyed by all traffic on public roads.
A   Pedestrians wait.   B   Pedestrians cross now.
1   RED means STOP
2   RED and AMBER means STOP but be ready to proceed when green
    appears.
3   GREEN means PROCEED if safe to do so.
4   AMBER means STOP unless too close to stop-line.
5   GREEN ARROW means proceed only in direction indicated.

1. If there is no policeman controlling the crossing, you have the right to cross at any time, *but always be sure to give approaching traffic time to stop*. This is particularly important on wet days, because if you cause a motorist to put on his brakes suddenly he may skid right into you.

2.   If there *is* a policeman or traffic warden controlling the crossing, you must wait until he stops the traffic for you before you step off the kerb.

At other kinds of crossing you must obey the lights or the signals given by a policeman. If the crossing is not controlled in any way, you may cross only when the road is clear – traffic is not bound to stop for you.

Further Reading

The Observer Pocket Series (Warne).
I – Spy British Wild Animals (Dickens Press).
I – Spy in the Hedgerow (Dickens Press).
Map Reading for the Countrygoer (Ramblers' Association).
Understanding Maps, Nancy Scott (Wills and Hepworth).
Know the Game – Map Reading (Educational Productions).
The Hike Book, J. Cox (Lutterworth).
Art of Cycling, N. Spencer (Thorsons).
The Highway Code (HMSO).

In the Home

Illness often strikes as suddenly as an accident. What would you do if your mother were taken ill or had an accident and she had to spend a few days in bed or had to go into hospital for treatment? Would you be able to look after her and the rest of the family? This chapter has been planned partly with such a situation in mind. There are ideas for easy meals for you to prepare for the rest of the family, for sick-room cookery and guidance on nursing someone who is ill in bed. You will also find some notes on elementary first aid and how to deal with various emergencies.

Just as it is important that you should have practical knowledge of first aid if you are to deal with an accident, so too should you know how to cook before you have to. Why not try some of the recipes on the following pages next time your mother is not too busy in the kitchen?

Cookery

Oven Chart

You will find many useful and tasty recipes in old cookery books, but may be puzzled in these days of thermostatically controlled ovens by references to a 'very hot' or 'moderate' oven. The following are the corresponding temperatures and thermostat marks.

	Electric ° F	Gas Mark
Very hot	500	9
Hot	450–475	7–8
Fairly hot	400–425	6
Moderate	350–375	4–5
Slow	300–350	2–3
Very slow	250–275	$\frac{1}{4}$–1

Handy Measures

Some recipes still give quantities of ingredients in teacups, breakfast-cups, teaspoons and tablespoons. Although you will get far more accurate quantities and are more likely to produce good results by weighing out solids and measuring liquids in fluid ounces or parts of a pint, the following are the approximate equivalents of the older measures – approximate because the capacity of cups and spoons vary so much.

Liquid Ingredients

1 small teacupful	$\frac{1}{4}$ pint (gill) or 5 fluid oz.
1 breakfastcupful or 1 tumbler	$\frac{1}{2}$ pint or 10 fluid oz.
1 tablespoonful (3 teaspoonfuls)	$\frac{1}{2}$ fluid oz.
1 teaspoonful	60 drops
$1\frac{1}{4}$ lb. (20 oz.)	1 pint, 20 fluid oz.

Solid Ingredients

Ingredient	Quantity	Weight
Breadcrumbs	2 heaped tablespoonsful	1 oz.
Flour, finely chopped suet	1 heaped tablespoonful	1 oz.
Sugar, salt, rice	1 level tablespoonful	1 oz.
Syrup *or* jam	1 level tablespoonful	2 oz.
Syrup *or* jam	1 breakfastcupful	8 oz.
Egg	1	2 oz. (approx.)
Flour	1 level teacupful	4 oz.

Weights

3 halfpennies	$\frac{1}{2}$ oz.
3 pennies *or* 6 halfpennies	1 oz.

Easy Recipes

Greek Shepherd's Pie

1 lb minced beef.
1 large onion
1 tablespoonful oil

Large or small tin of tomatoes
3 eggs
2 oz. cheese (if desired)

Chop onion and fry in a little oil. Add mince and fry a little more. Add tomatoes and warm all together. Put in greased dish. Beat up eggs and pour in top.
Sprinkle with cheese if desired. Cook in moderate oven for 25–30 minutes. (Electric: 350° F; Gas: mark 4.)

Chicken and Mushroom Casserole (for 4 persons)

$\frac{3}{4}$ pint milk
4 chicken joints
$1\frac{1}{2}$ oz. mushrooms
1 oz. butter or margarine

2 oz. streaky bacon
1 large onion peeled and sliced
1 oz. flour
Salt and pepper

Fry chicken joints in the butter until golden brown on all sides, and place in large casserole.

Slice mushrooms, dice bacon and fry both together with onions in the butter left from chicken and place in casserole.

Stir flour into remaining butter, gradually blend in milk, bring to boil stirring constantly. Season well and pour over chicken. Cook in moderately hot oven (Electric: 350° F.; Gas: mark 4) until chicken is cooked (1½ hours).

Fidgety Pie

Equal quantity of apples, onions, bacon and cheese. Chop or grate all ingredients. Add water to moisten, and pepper, salt and sugar to taste. Bake in a fireproof dish in a moderate oven (Electric: 350° F.; Gas: mark 4) for 20–30 minutes until brown.

Apple Crumble

5 oz. self-raising flour	1 lb. cooking apples
2 oz. sugar	2 oz. margarine
Pinch of salt	

Put flour, sugar and salt into bowl. Rub margarine in until the mixture resembles fine bread crumbs. Peel, core and slice apples. Put apples into bottom of dish, spread mixture over the apples, bake in a moderate oven (Electric: 380° F.; Gas: mark 5) until golden brown.

Sponge Pudding

4 oz. self-raising flour	2 oz. sugar
2 oz. margarine	Pinch of salt
1 egg	A little milk

Put sugar, salt and flour into a bowl. Rub in the margarine and mix well with egg and milk. Put into a greased basin and steam for 1½ hours. Serve with custard. This basic pudding can be varied by adding sultanas or currants, or by putting jam or syrup at the bottom of the basin.

Lemon Sago Pudding

1½ pints milk	2½ oz. sago
1½ oz. sugar	Grated rind of 1 medium lemon

Grease a 2-pint ovenproof dish. Put the milk in a saucepan, bring to boil, and sprinkle in the sago and sugar stirring all the time.

Simmer for 10–15 minutes, or until the mixture thickens. Stir in lemon rind; pour into the prepared dish.

Bake in lower part of pre-heated oven (Electric: 425° F.; Gas: mark 6) for 30 minutes, or until a golden colour. Serve hot with cream, if liked.

Macaroons

6 oz. caster sugar
2 egg whites

6 oz. desiccated coconut

Beat the egg whites stiff with a fork or whisk, then add the sugar and coconut. Put teaspoonsful on to rice paper or greaseproof paper and bake at 300° F. (Gas: mark 2) until golden brown.

Munch

10 oz. rolled oats
5 oz. demerara sugar
7 oz. margarine

1 tablespoonful syrup
1 pinch of salt
2 or 3 drops almond essence

Melt margarine, sugar and syrup together in a saucepan and add essence. (*Do not let the mixture boil.*) When all the mixture has melted add the oats. Spread in a shallow tin, and bake in a cool oven 300° F. (Gas: mark 2) for about ¾ hour until golden grown. Mark in fingers or squares. Leave until cold before turning out.

Toffee Making

(*A cooking thermometer is quite useful to have while making toffee but it is not absolutely essential.*)

Old-fashioned Treacle Toffee

2 cupfuls treacle
½ teaspoonful lemon juice

½ teaspoonful bicarbonate of soda

Boil treacle in a large saucepan until it hardens when a spoonful is dropped in a cup of cold water. Stir it all the time over a fairly low heat. And the bicarbonate and lemon juice and at once pour into a well-buttered tin. When it is cold enough to handle pull the toffee until it becomes a light yellow, then cut into pieces.

Victoria Toffee

1 lb. brown sugar
¼ pint water
1 teaspoonful vinegar

2 small tablespoonfuls of treacle
1½ oz. butter
A pinch of cream of tartar

Add the water to the sugar in a saucepan. Dissolve the sugar then add the rest of the ingredients. Boil up to 290° F. stirring occasionally. Pour toffee into a well-buttered tin, mark in squares and when set break into pieces.

Uncooked Coconut Ice

4 tablespoonsful condensed milk
12 oz. icing sugar

6 oz. desiccated coconut
Drop of cochineal

Mix together the condensed milk and icing sugar.
Stir in the coconut. The mixture should be very stiff.
Divide into two parts. Tint one-half of the mixture pale pink with cochineal.
Shape the mixture into two indentical bars and press firmly together.
Dust a tin or plate with icing sugar and leave the coconut ice on this until firm.

Sick-room Cookery

Sick people do not usually feel like eating and for this reason food should be served in small portions and in the most attractive manner possible, to tempt them.
Food for invalids should always be fresh and of the best quality. Give as much variety as possible, studying their likes and dislikes. It should always be cooked in the most simple way; steaming, boiling, grilling or baking. Highly seasoned dishes and fried foods are unsuitable.

Egg Jelly

$\frac{1}{2}$ pint liquid made up of the strained juice of 1 lemon and water
Peel of a lemon, thinly cut
1 egg

2 oz. sugar, or to taste
$\frac{1}{4}$ oz. gelatine

Put all ingredients except the egg into a saucepan. Beat the egg and add it, beating all the time. Stir with a fork over very low heat until the gelatine is dissolved. *The mixture must not boil.* Cool, strain, and put into a mould and when set turn out on to a dish.

Bread and Butter Pudding

$\frac{1}{2}$ pint milk
1 dessertspoonful sugar
2 or 3 slices of bread and butter

1 egg
1 tablespoonful of clean sultanas
Nutmeg

Grease pie dish well. Beat egg and milk together. Place bread and butter in dish (butter side down), sprinkle sultanas over, then another layer of bread and butter. Pour custard over, stand aside for $\frac{1}{2}$ hour. Grate nutmeg over, if liked. Stand in tin of water, bake slowly until custard is set on top, and a pale brown in colour. Serve immediately.

Scrambled Egg

1 or 2 new-laid eggs
1 dessertspoonful milk
Pepper and salt

Piece of butter
Slice of hot buttered toast

Make toast, butter it, and keep it hot. Beat eggs with a little milk. Add pepper and salt. Melt butter in saucepan, pour in egg mixture and cook slowly, stirring well until the egg is nearly set. Pile on the toast, garnish with parsley. Serve at once.

Steamed Fish in Parsley Sauce

If necessary fillet and skin the fish. Lay fish on board, skinned side up, season, squeeze a few drops of lemon juice over and roll up. Grease a soup plate, place fish on it, cover with a greased paper and a saucepan lid. Place over a saucepan of boiling water, cook for about 20 minutes. Liquid from the fish should be used for the sauce, making up the required quantity of fluid with milk.

Sauce
½ oz. butter
½ oz. flour
1 teaspoonful of chopped parsley

7 oz. liquid (milk or milk and liquid from fish)

Melt the butter in a small saucepan. Remove from heat and stir in the flour. Return the saucepan to the heat, and cook slowly for 6 minutes, but do not brown. Add liquid slowly, beating well until free from lumps. Bring to the boil, stirring all the time, and boil for 3 minutes. Add chopped parsley. Coat the fish and serve.

Chicken

Give the breast as this is the most tender. Stew gently with milk until tender using a double saucepan. Serve with mashed potatoes.

Poached Egg

These are light and easily digestible.
If a poacher is not available:
Pour water into a frying-pan, or small saucepan, enough to cover the egg. Add a level teaspoonful of salt and a teaspoonful of vinegar to each pint of water.
Bring the water to the boil, and then allow to SIMMER.
Break an egg into a cup, being careful not to break the yoke and slide it gently into the water.

Make sure the water is only simmering. Tilt the pan and with a tablespoon gently gather the white together round the yolk. Simmer for 3 minutes or until the whites are set.

Lift out with a fish slice, drain and serve on hot buttered toast.

Baked Custard

3 eggs	1 oz. sugar
1 pint milk	Vanilla essence
Nutmeg	

Mix milk with sugar, heat until dissolved. Pour on to lightly beaten eggs. Mix in vanilla essence.

Strain into lightly greased dish, sprinkle with grated nutmeg. Bake in a moderate oven (Electric: 350° F.; Gas: mark 4) for 45 minutes.

First Aid

The Vital First Minutes

Have you ever been a witness of an accident and seen others gaze numbed by the shock of what they see, trying to think what to do, or wasting precious minutes searching for dressings when the victim is bleeding to death? By learning a few basic rules you could well help to save someone's life. (N.B. Always call for a doctor as soon as possible.)

Bleeding

1 Unless the person is not breathing, you should stop bleeding before treating any other injury.

2 Make the person lie down, and raise the bleeding part (unless it is fractured).

3 Apply pressure:

Direct with a pad plus your two thumbs pressing on top of each other on the exact spot which is bleeding.

Indirect by pressing on the nearest pressure point.

Venous bleeding: Venous blood *flows* from the wound and is dark red in colour. Such bleeding would occur in a burst varicose vein, usually at the ankle. Treat by:

1 Raising the limb.

2 Placing a firm pad (containing a penny) over the wound.

3 Bandaging tightly and sending for a doctor.

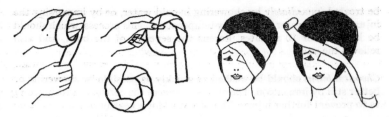

Fig. 10. Glass wound – the ring pad.   Fig. 11. Dressing for injured eye.

Arterial bleeding: Arterial blood *spurts* out and is bright red in colour. This bleeding is the most serious type and will soak through any pad. Never remove the original pad, but apply another on top. You may need several on top of one another. Otherwise treat as above.

Nose Bleeding
1 Sit the person down with her head bent forward.
2 Pinch the bridge of the person's nose and tell her to breath through her mouth.
3 Undo any tight clothing around the person's neck.
4 On no account attempt to plug a bleeding nose.
5 If bleeding continues after 20 minutes send for a doctor.

Glass Wound
1 Never try to remove glass which has penetrated into the flesh.
2 Clean the wound superficially, apply a firm ring pad (*see Figure 10*) and bandage it firmly into position.
3 Otherwise treat in the same way as for other types of bleeding.

Dressing for Injured Eye
However painful an eye injury may be, never try to remove anything embedded in the surface of the eye as this could make the injury worse. Instead put on pad over the eye, bandage it very lightly in position and get expert help as soon as possible. Use a built-up dressing on the eye if necessary. *See Figure 11.*

Burns and Scalds
Burns are caused by dry heat and scalds by hot liquids or by steam. Small, deep burns are much less serious than large superficial ones.

Burns caused by hot objects or by rubbing, e.g. sliding down a rope, should be treated *immediately* by showering in cold water, or by immersing the injured part in water below body temperature. This process, which should be kept up for 10 minutes, lessens the severity of the burn, and also relieves the pain.

Chemical burns should be washed as quickly as possible by showering or better still by immersion. The aim is to *remove* the corrosive substance so as to prevent further injury. Then treat as for a heat burn.

1   *Preventing infection*. The skin acts as a protective covering for the body. When the skin is burnt, germs are likely to enter and multiply in the damaged tissue. Cover the burnt area with a sterile dressing larger than the affected area. *Do not use cotton wool or hairy lint*. As burnt clothes stick to the skin, *leave them in place*.
2   Place the sterile dressing quickly over the clothes trying to cover one small area at a time, rather than doing it all at once.
3   Conscious burnt patients should be given drinks of water, but remember *do not* give fluid by mouth to an unconscious person.
4   *Reassure the casualty*. Try to remain calm and make her as comfortable as possible. A burnt person is terrified, thinking she is going to die or be scarred for life, so tell her that she is in good hands.
5   *Get the casualty to hospital as quickly as possible*. Superficial (surface) burns are usually very painful, while deep burns may not be so painful because the nerves which carry the sensation of pain have been destroyed.

Scalds should be treated *at once* by showering or immersion in cold water. If the victim's clothing is soaked, but not stuck to her skin, remove the clothing. Then treat as for a heat burn.

Artificial Respiration
Electric shock, gassing and drowning frequently stop the victim's breathing, and as such accidents happen suddenly, it is essential that you know exactly how to set about reviving the victim and that you have practised on a dummy for you to save her life.

The modern method of giving artificial respiration is to breath air directly into the victim's lungs. (This method has replaced former methods of pressing the lungs because it is far more efficient in ventilating the lungs and starting natural breathing once more.) There are three variants to the technique – mouth to nose, mouth to mouth, or for babies and small children mouth to nose and mouth. For adults mouth to nose is most successful because there is less danger of inflating the victim's stomach.

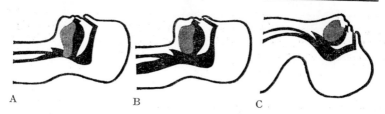

Fig. 12. Mouth to mouth respiration. These three diagrams show why the position of the casualty's head is vital. A. In an unconscious casualty the tongue may block the throat: B. Normal clear airway in a conscious person: C. In the head fully back position, the air passages are clear and unobstructed.

1   Pull the victim's head as far back as it will go and remove her dentures or any foreign matter that may be in her mouth.

2   Move air in and out of her lungs by blowing slowly into her nose, while preventing air from escaping from her mouth by covering it firmly. When the victim's chest rises remove your mouth from the victim's nose and allow air to escape from her lungs (see Figure 13).)

3   Continue blowing air into the victim's nose and letting it escape until the victim starts to breathe naturally, or for at least one hour.

4   When the victim begins to breathe her breaths will be shallow and weak. To improve the victim's breathing continue blowing into her nose, but take care that your breaths coincide with the victim's.

5   When the victim is breathing properly, turn her into the unconscious position (see Figure 13).

6   Watch the victim carefully and check that she continues to breath normally. Should her breathing fail again turn her on her back and start artificial respiration again.

7   The victim will have to go to hospital, but do not be in too much of a hurry to send her. See that she is continuing to breathe naturally first.

Electrical Accident

1   Switch off the current, if possible.

2   Insulate your own hand and feet (use leather gloves and rubber boots) before touching the patient.

3   Apply artificial respiration if breathing has stopped or is faltering.

4   Treat for shock and a superficial burn.

Whenever possible the current should be switched off, and also the faulty appliance disconnected from the main by removing the plug. If you do not know the position of the switch, you must take precautions before

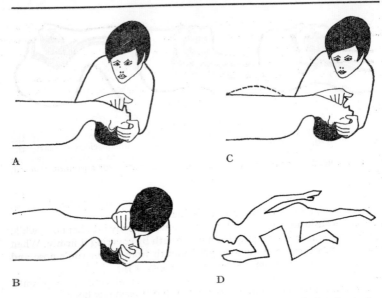

Fig. 13. Mouth to nose respiration. A. Head fully back: B. Inflate lungs by blowing into nose: C. Watch chest falling: D. Unconscious person position.

attempting to pull the victim clear. You must use some insulating material, e.g. rubber or dry wood (anything wet will conduct electricity). If you are not already wearing rubber soled shoes, stand on a rubber mat or piece of dry wood and if possible, make use of a walking stick or broom handle (never an umbrella) to drag the victim clear. If you cannot find a stick quickly, then protect your hands with rubber gloves, mackintosh, thickness of dry clothing, or dry newspaper.

Ice Accident
1 If the victim is visible, tie a sharp pointed object to a rope and slide this across the ice, instructing the victim to hold on to the ice with the spike.
2 Failing this try to get a rope, ladder or plank across the hole, or make a human chain of people lying on the ice to lift the victim out of the water. Pull the victim clear across the ice face downwards.
3 If there is no sign of the victim, make sure the rescuer (even a good swimmer) has a life line tied round her waist before starting to search.

4   If the victim has stopped breathing apply mouth to nose respiration and treat for shock.

Fire Accidents

Clothing on Fire is a common cause of severe burns. If clothes catch alight push the victim to the ground with burning area uppermost and smother the flames with a rug, blanket or door-mat. Once the flames are extinguished treat the burns.

House on Fire

1   Warn the occupants whose lives may be in danger.
2   Know how to call the fire brigade and be able to give short, clear messages.
3   Anyone who has been involved in a fire needs to be treated for shock.

Home Nursing

When nursing someone REMEMBER:
1   To write down and report to the doctor any change in the person's condition.
2   To follow the doctor's instructions carefully.
3   To move and speak carefully and calmly.
4   To see that meals are well served and that the tray looks attractive and appetizing.
5   To make the person as comfortable as possible, by shaking flattened pillows and smoothing creases in the undersheet.

Sick Room

Make the best of the person's usual room. If there is a choice pick a light, airy room, unless the doctor says otherwise.

Preparing the room. Surroundings make a great difference to a person who is ill, so add such things as a vase of flowers or a brightly coloured picture.

The room should be swept, brushed or mopped, and all furniture dusted with a damp duster. It is important to prevent as much as possible of the dust from flying about. Ventilate the room at least twice daily to let in a fresh supply of clean air.

Improvising Extra Comforts

Back rest. This is a great help if the person is to be kept in a sitting position, and can be made by turning an ordinary wooden chair, with its seat over the edge of the bed, and the back of it forming a slope for the person to lean against. It must be, of course, well padded with pillows or cushions.

Bed jacket. When sitting up in bed a patient should wear something extra. A cardigan makes a good substitute for a bed jacket and requires less effort to slip on and off than a dressing-gown.

Bells. A small hand bell may not be heard downstairs, but one suspended from the banister on the end of a length of string may serve the purpose better. The sound of a whistle is more effective.

Foot cradles. The object of these is to take the pressure of the bedclothes off one or both legs. A small, low three-legged stool placed over one leg, or a cardboard box with the ends taken out may be adequate.

Washing the Patient
Have the water at a temperature of about 100° F. Place soap and flannel or sponge on a large plate or in a shallow dish. Have talcum powder and a large puff handy. See that a warm towel is near.

Close the windows and turn on the fire, if there is one.

Encourage the patient to wash herself, standing ready with water, soap, and so on, to be handed to her as required.

If the patient cannot wash herself, wash her face, neck and ears first, placing an old clean towel on the pillow beforehand. Then draw back the bedclothes, place an old blanket under and over her, and, uncovering her to the waist, wash and dry her, back and front. That done, cover her body and uncover one of her legs, washing and drying it. Then cover it and uncover, wash and dry the other leg. Finally remove the old blankets and make her comfortable again. Give her a brush and comb, and cosmetics if she asks for them.

Giving Medicines
1   Read the directions on the bottle and listen carefully to any instructions given by the doctor.
2   Using a clean medicine glass hold the glass and bottle at eye level and pour out *exactly* the quantity stated in the directions. Always pour with the label uppermost and replace the cork of the bottle after pouring out.
3   If a pill is to be taken, have a glass of water handy. Tell the patient to put the pill as far on to the back of her tongue as possible, then take a good drink. The pill will slip down practically unnoticed.

If for any reason one dose is missed, do *not* give a double dose next time. Never give the patient chocolate or anything similar 'to take the taste away' unless the doctor gives permission.

Child Care

It is a great responsibility to take charge of a child, because the mother relies on you to keep the child out of danger.

How to prevent accidents to a child in house or garden.
1   A child should never be left alone in a room with an unguarded fire.
2   Handles of saucepans and spouts of kettles on the stove, should be turned inwards so that he cannot grab them and get scalded from boiling water spilling over.
3   See that he understands not to play with electric switches, and gas taps.
4   Medicines and tablets should be locked up out of reach.
5   Matches, razor blades, knives, should not be left where he can get them.
6   Make sure all rusty nails have been removed from boxes, before the child is allowed to play with them.
7   Securely close the garden gate before the child goes into the garden.
8   A child should never be left alone in an upstairs room with the window open unless there are bars at the window.
9   Be especially careful if there is water about. A child can drown in a few inches of water.

Telephoning
For police, fire or ambulance.
When an accident has happened always telephone the police, by dialling 999 or following local emergency procedure. The police will contact the doctor and ambulance. Give the address where the accident occurred and explain what has happened. Reassure the patient and make her comfortable. Write down any message the patient may give you.

Animal Emergencies

Animals in a Fire
Animals are difficult to rescue from fire, because they become very frightened. Cattle may be driven out, but horses and ponies will not move unless they are blindfolded. Quickly tie a sack over their eyes before trying to get them out of a burning stable or barn.

Animals Stranded in Floods

Rapidly rising flood water is the usual cause of the loss of animals, who are caught in the fields and surrounded by ever deepening water. Raise the alarm, driving all animals towards an escape route, if there still is one, or the highest piece of ground. Cattle and horses will swim behind a boat, held by ropes behind their horns or a halter.

Animals Caught by Wire

Rusty barbed wire is most dangerous. Do not frighten the animal caught on it. Move quietly and gently, and try to gain his confidence. Never take the animal from the wire, always take the wire off the animal.

Horse or Pony Involved in a Road Accident

A veterinary surgeon should be called in all but the slightest accidents. The animal should be kept as still as possible and traffic directed round it if possible. If a horse being driven with a harness slips on a greasy or frozen road, he will begin to kick at once. Sit on his head! You need not be afraid of doing this, he will lie quietly, especially if his eyes are covered. Someone who understands can then cut away the harness and drag away the cart. Put sand on the road, so that when the horse attempts to get up he will not slip again.

Leading a Frightened Animal

The animal should be led by his owner or someone whom he knows. He should be led by a short rein, and not given a free head. It is much easier to lead a horse if blindfolded. A gentle pat on the neck and reassuring words in his ears can help a great deal. Keep about his shoulder level, not in front or he will tread on you, or behind or you are asking for a kick.

Further Reading

Modern Living Series: Your Health, Your Food, Mary Davis Peters (Longmans).

Cooking, Sylvia Duncan (Michael Joseph).

Come into the Kitchen: Cooking for boys and girls, A. Gordon (Gollancz).

Birds Eye Book of Britain's Favourite Recipes, Ambrose Heath (Wolfe).

500 Recipes for Sweets and Candies, Marguerite Patten (Paul Hamlyn).

British Red Cross Society Manuals – *Junior First Aid, Junior Nursing*.

St. John Ambulance Brigade Manuals – *Basic First Aid, Preliminary Home Nursing*.

Essential First Aid, A. Ward Gardner and Peter J. Roylance (Pan Books).

Needlework

By reading this chapter you will not learn how to knit, embroider or crochet; however it will provide reminders of how to do the different stitches, and of some of the basic steps in dressmaking.

All the topics covered in this chapter involve practice and developing a technique, things which you can only learn from someone who is experienced. So if you run into difficulties do not hesitate to get help before you spoil the article.

Knitting

Wool

Wools are sold in different 'plys', that is with a different number of strands, 1 ply being one strand (only used for knitting very fine lace), 2 ply having two strands twisted together, 3 ply three strands, etc. Good wool should feel soft to the touch and should be elastic.

Needles

The larger needles have the lowest numbers, e.g. number 6 is larger than number 7. Larger needles should be used for thicker wool. Different people knit with different degrees of tightness and in consequence need different needles to produce similar work, but the average person will use 10 or 11 for 3 ply and 8 or 9 for 4 ply.

Patterns

Most leading wool manufacturers issue booklets giving useful instructions and advice suitable for use with their own wools. Any wool shop will have good simple books of directions for all kinds of knitted articles.

Casting On

1   Make a slip knot and place the loop on the left-hand needle.
2   Place the point of the right-hand needle in the loop also, holding the wool in the right hand.
3   Place the wool over the forefinger of the right hand and round the point of the right-hand needle.
4   Draw the wool through the loop on the left-hand needle, thus forming a second loop.
5   Slip this loop on to the left-hand needle.
6   Repeat 3, 4 and 5 until you have the required number of stitches.
(See Figure 14.)

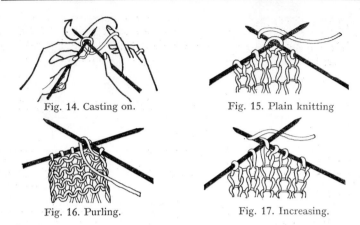

Fig. 14. Casting on.

Fig. 15. Plain knitting

Fig. 16. Purling.

Fig. 17. Increasing.

Plain Knitting

1   Place the point of the right-hand needle in the first stitch of the left-hand needle. (*See Figure 15.*)
2   Holding the wool in the right hand, wrap it round the point of the right-hand needle.
3   Draw the wool through the first stitch on the left-hand needle.
4   Drop the first stitch off the left-hand needle on to right-hand needle.
5   Repeat this action until all the stitches are worked on to the right-hand needle.

Purling

1   Place the point of the right-hand needle through the front of the first stitch on the left-hand needle.
2   Wrap the wool round the point of the right-hand needle and draw a loop through the first stitch on the left-hand needle.
3   Drop the first stitch off the left-hand needle on to the right-hand needle.
4   Repeat this action until all the stitches are worked on to the right-hand needle. (*See Figure 16.*)

Increasing

1   Knit the stitch in the usual way, but do not drop it off the left-hand needle.
2   Place the point of the right-hand needle into the back of the same stitch and knit again into the stitch.
3   Slip the stitch off the left-hand needle. Two stitches will thus have been formed out of the one stitch. (*See Figure 17.*)

106

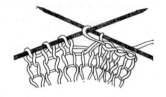

Fig. 18. Casting off.

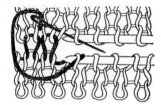

Fig. 19. Grafting.

Decreasing

Slip the point of the right-hand needle through *two* stitches instead of one and knit the two stitches off the left-hand needle in the usual way.

Casting Off

1 Knit the first two stitches in the usual way.
2 Place the point of the left-hand needle into the second stitch on the right-hand needle (i.e. the first stitch knitted).
3 Draw this stitch over the first stitch (i.e. the second stitch knitted).
4 Knit the next stitch so that there are two stitches on the right-hand needle again and repeat until all the stitches are cast off.
5 When the last stitch is reached break off the wool and draw the end of the wool through the stitch. (*See Figure 18.*)

Grafting

This is used for joining together two pieces of knitting to avoid a ridged seam, mainly for the toes of socks and the shoulder-seams of pullovers and jumpers.

1 No stitches are cast off: they are left on the needle.
2 Leave an end of wool for grafting on one of the pieces of knitting to be joined.
3 Thread this end of wool through a wool needle.
4 Place the two portions of knitting together with the right side of the work facing you.
5 Insert the needle into the first stitch of the front needle as if for knitting.
6 Draw it through the stitch and slip the stitch off the needle.
7 Insert the needle into the second stitch of the front needle as if for purling.
8 Draw the wool through but let the stitch remain on the needle.
9 Take the wool under the front needle and insert the wool needle into the first stitch of the back needle, as if for purling.

107

10 Draw the wool through this stitch and slip the stitch off the needle.

11 Insert the needle into the second stitch of the back needle as if for knitting.

12 Draw the wool through the stitch and let the stitch remain on the needle.

13 Bring the wool forward under the needle and repeat from 5 until all stitches are worked off.

14 Darn in the end of wool securely. (*See Figure 19.*)

Crocheting

*(Abbreviations: ch. – chain stitch; s.c. – single crochet; d.c. – double crochet h.tr. – half treble; tr. – treble; l.tr. – long treble; * sign of repetition)*

Holding the Wool and Hook

Holding the hook between the first finger and the thumb of the right hand and letting the second finger rest near the point of the hook, make a slip loop and pass it on to the hook. Holding the work, as it is formed, between the first finger and thumb of the left hand, pass the wool from the ball over the first and second fingers, under the third and round the little finger. (*See Figure 20.*)

Chain Stitch

This is used for starting all crochet work.

Holding the wool and the hook as described above and making a slip loop with which to commence, * pass the hook from left to right under the wool (held in the left hand), draw this thread through the loop already on the hook and repeat from * for the length required (*See Figure 20B.*)

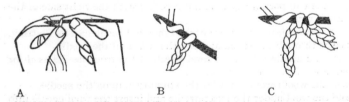

A   B   C

Fig. 20. Crochet. A. Position of hands: B. Chain stitch: C. Single crochet.

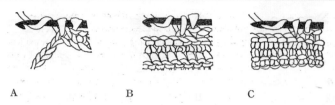

Fig. 21. A. Double crochet: B. Flat surface: C. Ridged surface.

Single Crochet (or slip stitch)
This is used chiefly for joining or in fancy patterns, and is the shortest (in height) of all crochet stitches.

Make the required length of chain (ch.).

1st row – Miss the end ch. (near the hook), * pass the hook through the next ch., draw the wool through both the stitches on the hook, repeat from * to the end of the ch., 1 ch., turn.

Repeat further rows for the length required. (*See Figure 20C.*)

Double Crochet
This usually requires to be worked firmly, evenly and with medium tension.

Make the required length of chain.

1st row – Miss 2 ch., * draw a loop through the next ch., then draw a loop through both the stitches on the hook, repeat from * to the end of the row, 2 ch., turn.

2nd row – (The 2 ch. at the turning of the previous row forms the 1st stitch.) * Draw a loop through the next d.c., draw a loop through both stitches on the hook, repeat from * to the end of row, 2 ch., turn.

Repeat the 2nd row for the length required.

Two different effects can be obtained from the above stitch:

A flat surface is produced by, for each new stitch, inserting the hook through *the two threads* forming a chain along the top edge of the previous row.

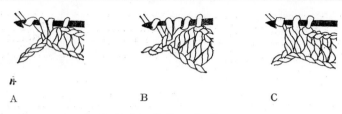

Fig. 22. A. Half treble: B. Treble: C. Long treble.

A ridged surface is produced by, for each new stitch, inserting the hook *through the back thread* of the stitches that lie along the top edge of the previous row. (*See Figure 21.*)

Half Treble
Make the required length of chain.

1st row – Miss 3 ch., * pass the wool round the hook, draw a loop through the next ch., draw a loop through all the 3 stitches on the hook, repeat from * to the end of the row, 3 ch., turn.

2nd row – (The 3 ch. at the turning of the previous row forms the 1st stitch.) * Pass the wool round the hook, draw a loop through the next h.tr., draw a loop through all the 3 stitches on the hook, repeat from * to the end of the row, 3 ch., turn.

Repeat the 2nd row for the length required. (*See Figure 22.*)

Joining the Wool
When only a few inches of wool are left, take the end from the new ball of wool and complete the last stitch with this. Continue working over both ends of wool for several stitches, afterwards continuing with the new thread.

Increasing
In plain fabric, work 2 stitches on to one. In the case of a fancy stitch, work 2 pattern groups into one. (Detailed instructions for this are usually given on the patterns.)

Decreasing
In plain fabric, the usual method is to miss a stitch, while in a fancy pattern special instructions are always given in the pattern.

Embroidery Fig. 23

If you have to buy materials it is wiser to choose to make a small article from good quality materials than a larger article for which you may have to make do with second best quality material.

Always make sure your needle suits your thread, and that it is sharp and free from rust. If you have an embroidery frame, use it, as it helps to keep the tension of your stitches more even, and avoid puckering the material.

Begin your work with two or three small stitches, at the back, near where you are going to start, then bring your needle through to the front.

Running Stitch
This stitch is made by going under and over an equal amount of material.

Back Stitch
Bring your needle out and take one stitch backwards, bringing your needle out again an equal distance from the other stitch.

Cross Stitch
This is worked by counting threads: count three to six threads according to material, make one row of slanting stitches, and then work back again, crossing the first row with a second row slanting in the opposite direction.

Satin Stitch
This stitch is made by sewing a series of stroke stitches so closely side by side that none of the fabric shows between them.
1   Bring the needle through to the right side on one edge of the outline to be filled.
2   Put the needle in again exactly opposite on the other edge of the outline, making a straight line of thread across the space.
3   Bring the needle up again as close as possible to the start of the first stitch, and so on until the space is filled.

Stem Stitch
This outline stitch is used for working stems and leaf-veins. Work from the bottom of the line upwards, keeping the thread always to one side of the needle.

Blanket Stitch
The stitch is worked from left to right.

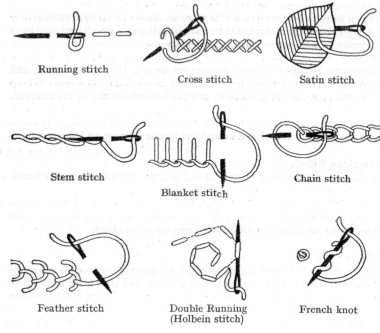

Running stitch

Cross stitch

Satin stitch

Stem stitch

Blanket stitch

Chain stitch

Feather stitch

Double Running (Holbein stitch)

French knot

Fig. 23. Some embroidery stitches.

1   Hold the thread down with the thumb.
2   Place the needle through the material at right-angles to the direction of the thread.
3   Draw the needle through over the thread.
4   Pull up the thread, thus forming a bar along the edge.

Chain Stitch

Work this stitch downwards or towards yourself.
1   Bring the needle up from the wrong side at the top of the line or design.
2   Put the needle in close to where it came up, holding the thread down under the needle to form a loop.
3   Pull up the thread.

4   Insert the needle inside the loop, bringing it out again a little lower down. Repeat.

Chain stitch should be worked loosely to avoid puckering the material, and the stitches should be of an even size. A single chain stitch is known as *Lazy Daisy Stitch*.

Feather Stitch
This stitch is formed by blanket stitch worked first to the right and then to the left, the stitches being below each other instead of alongside.

Double Running (Holbein stitch)
This is worked in two journeys along the line. First make a row of running stitches, turn round and make a second row of stitches, in the spaces left on the first journey.

French Knot
1   Bring the needle up to the right side and pick up a tiny piece of material where the knot is to be.
2   Twist the thread once, twice, or three times (according to the size of knot required) round the needle.
3   Pull the needle through, holding the thread down with the left thumb. The thread will now form a knot.

Dressmaking

Before committing yourself to making a particular dress make yourself familiar with different types of patterns. Choose simple ones to start with. Before deciding on the quantity of material required make sure by using a tape measure that you have the necessary measurements of the figure, for which the garment is to be made. As long as it is not too bulky, measurements may be taken over the wearer's dress.

Order of Taking Measurements
Bust Measurement
1   Place the tape-measure round the largest part of the figure, keeping it well up at the back because of the width of the back.
2   See that the tape-measure is not too tight.
Waist Measurement
1   Place the tape-measure round the natural waist-line.
2   Hold the measure firmly if a petersham band is to be fitted.
3   See that the tape-measure is not held too tightly for a dress or blouse.

Hip Measurement

Take this measurement twice:

1   At the largest part of the figure – usually 8 in. down from the waist-line, although this will vary slightly with tall and short figures.

2   Level with the hip-bones – usually 3 to 4 in. below the waist-line.

This double measurement is important because of the great difference in figures.

Shoulder to Waist – Front

Place the tape-measure to the top of the shoulder close to the neck and measure over the bust to the natural waist-line.

Shoulder to Ground – Front

Place the tape-measure to the top of the shoulder and measure over the bust to the ground.

Across the Chest

Measure across the chest 2 in. below the base of the throat from arm-hole to arm-hole.

Shoulder to Waist – Back

Place the tape-measure to the top of the shoulder close to the neck and measure over the shoulder-blades to the natural waist-line.

Shoulder to Ground – Back

Place the tape-measure to the top of the shoulder and measure to the ground.

Across the Back

Measure across the back from arm-hole to arm-hole.

Sleeve – Back Length

Flex the arm, and measure 2 in. below the shoulder at the arm-hole line, over the elbow to 1 in. beyond the wrist-bone.

Sleeve – Inside Length

Stretch out the arm and measure from the inside of the wrist to the arm-pit.

Elbow

Flex the arm and measure round the elbow and fore-arm.

Upper Arm

Relax the arm and measure round the thick part of the arm and above the elbow.

Wrist

Measure round the wrist.

Length of Dress

Decide the distance from the ground to the hem-line, i.e. the length of the dress, and take the measurements. Always check the measurements from time to time, as the human figure changes, especially that of the adolescent.

Patterns may seem complicated at first but if you study each piece carefully, you will see all are numbered and named. Large holes in the pattern often indicate the selvedge edge. See material is doubled carefully when a fold is indicated. Above all, read the instructions carefully even before unwrapping the material.

Cutting Out

Before you attempt to cut double, check that you have arranged all the necessary pieces of pattern, according to the instructions given for the width of material you are using.

Pin carefully, make sure the pins do not stick out beyond the pattern as these will obstruct the scissors. Grasp your scissors firmly, and make the first cut. Use the whole of the blade, not just the point. Always remember, when you see vv's cut out in the paper, that you **do not** cut them out in the material but mark with cotton, before removing the pattern. They are the guides for matching the pieces together.

Using a Sewing Machine

Sewing machines may be worked by hand, foot or electricity: work sewn by machine is done quickly, and is neat in appearance. To obtain good results it is necessary to understand how the machine works, especially how to wind the bobbin, thread the needle, alter the tension, and size of the stitch.

Do be careful: if in doubt on how to use the machine ask an adult to show you. If the machine is power driven be extremely careful in using it as you may have a nasty accident to a finger. Never let anyone help you by turning the handle of a machine – one person only should be in control of the machine.

Making Buttonholes

Depending upon their use ordinary sewn buttonholes have either straight or rounded ends. The most usual type has the end nearest to the edge of the garment rounded and the other straight. However, on shirts buttonholes for studs and cuff-links have both ends straight. Where a buttonhole is used as a slot for elastic or ribbon both ends must be rounded.

Buttonholes should be cut the way of the pull on the garment, otherwise the buttons will come undone. Buttonholes should be $\frac{1}{8}$ in. larger than the diameter of the button. Allow a little more if the button is ball-shaped.

To make the buttonhole first mark its position with two pins standing upright on the material. After cutting the material with sharp-pointed scissors, buttonhole stitch around the cut.

Darning

1 Match the thread with the fabric of the garment with respect to colour, texture and thickness.

2 Work on the wrong side of the fabric beginning at the bottom left-hand corner, working first away from you, and then towards you.

3 The darn should not leave any spaces between the stitches and should be flat and as neat as possible.

4 Remember it is better to darn a thin place before it wears into a hole.

Patching

Accidents may happen that make it necessary to put a patch on a garment to make it wearable. A burn or tear can be repaired with a piece of matching material. In addition, certain areas of garment are susceptible to excessive wear, for example a cotton dress may wear under the arm, but otherwise be in good condition. If the dress is not home-made and in consequence you do not have any spare pieces of the material, you could use a piece of the belt or a pocket to make a patch. If the material is a patterned one, the piece for the patch must match the pattern exactly and be put on to the right side of the dress, otherwise:

1 Tack on the wrong side of the garment a patch the edges of which have been turned once only.

2 Turn on to the right side and cut away the worn part being careful to keep the edges straight.

3 Make a narrow turning and sew all round the inner square.

4 Press the patch flat and remove the tacking threads.

Toymaking

Wool Balls and Birds

To make a wool ball, first collect scraps of wool, brightly coloured and of any length. Cut two equal circular discs from a piece of stiff cardboard, their diameters should be between 3 and 5 in. according to the size of ball. Place the discs together and cut a circular hole in the centre of each. Then wind wool through the central hole and over the ring until the hole is very tightly filled. Then take a sharp pair of scissors, insert the blade between the two layers of card and cut all round the edge of the outer circle. Do not let the wool slide from the central hole. When you have cut all the threads, slip a length of strong wool between the cards, wind it twice round the bundle of wool in the centre and tie very tightly. Finally, pull away the two card discs and trim to a perfect ball.

Animals such as rabbits, mice and chicks can be made by joining up several such balls. Use one ball for the head and one or two larger balls for the body.

Felt Animals

At first these are best made from a good pattern, but when you have gained some experience try making soft toys to your own designs. Most animals are made from three pieces.

Side pieces, which should follow a good silhouette of the animal. Always make these shapes as simple as possible. You will need two of these side pieces for each animal.

Under-body pieces, two for four-legged standing animals, but only one if the animal is to be sitting.

Head gusset, which is let into the top of the head and carried right down its back and also under the chin. You will need only one of these. Besides these three main parts, you will need such items as ears, tail, soles of feet, beaks and wings.

Eyes. Beads outlined with stitches make good eyes, but if the animal is intended for a young child it is safer to embroider the eyes or make them from felt.

Whiskers. These are best made from bristles.

Beaks. Cut out two pieces of material of the correct colour, stitch them together, stuff with scraps and sew them neatly on to the head.

When making felt animals to your own designs it is best to experiment with paper pieces before cutting the shapes out of felt.

Further Reading

Knitting Book, Mary Thomas (Hodder and Stoughton).
Your Book of Embroidery, J. B. Lumsden (Faber and Faber).
Embroidery Book, Mary Thomas (Hodder and Stoughton).
Home Dressmaking, A. M. Miall (Pitman).
Essentials of Modern Dressmaking, Winifred Parker and Dora Seton (Evans).
Soft Toy Making, Phyllis Chappell (Evans).

Sporting Records

Athletics
UK National Records

Event	Holder	Time min.	sec.
100 yards	D. Hyman		10·6
	H. Young		
220 yards	D. Arden		23·6
	M. Rand		
880 yards	A. Smith	2	04·2
1 mile	A. Smith	4	37·0
80 metres hurdles	B. Moore		10·5

Event	Holder	ft.	in.
High Jump	F. Slaap	5	9
Long Jump	M. Rand	22	2
Discus	S. Allday	156	6
Javelin	S. Platt	178	7½
Shot	S. Allday	49	1

(The above records are those which have been officially ratified at the time of going to press. However, as the ratification committees do not meet very often, it is quite likely that some of the above records have already been broken.)

Hockey

Results of International Matches

1950

England	3	v	Ireland	5
England	6	v	Scotland	2
England	11	v	Wales	1
England	1	v	Holland	0

1951

England	6	v	Ireland	1
England	8	v	Scotland	1
England	10	v	Wales	0

1952

England	1	v	Ireland	0
England	9	v	Scotland	2
England	12	v	Wales	2
England	2	v	Belgium	1

1953

England	5	v	Ireland	2
England	5	v	Scotland	2
England	6	v	Wales	2
England	11	v	Belgium	0

1954

England	5	v	Scotland	1
England	10	v	Wales	1
England	5	v	Ireland	0
England	12	v	Belgium	0

1955					England	2	v	Scotland	1
England	8	v	Ireland	0	England	0	v	Germany	2
England	6	v	Wales	1	1962				
England	7	v	Scotland	2	England	3	v	USA	3
England	4	v	Holland	1	England	3	v	Wales	1
1956					England	4	v	Scotland	2
England	6	v	USATT	0	England	0	v	Ireland	2
England	2	v	Ireland	1	England	2	v	Holland	2
England	4	v	Holland	1	1963				
England	6	v	Wales	0	England	0	v	Wales	1
England	5	v	Scotland	3	England	3	v	Ireland	0
1957					England	5	v	Scotland	0
England	6	v	Wales	0	England	0	v	Germany	0
England	2	v	Ireland	0	1964				
England	3	v	Scotland	1	England	1	v	Wales	1
England	1	v	Holland	0	England	3	v	Holland	2
1958					England	3	v	Scotland	2
England	5	v	Scotland	2	England	0	v	Ireland	1
England	2	v	Ireland	2	1965				
England	5	v	Wales	1	England	3	v	Wales	2
1959					England	1	v	S. Africa	3
England	8	v	Ireland	2	England	2	v	Scotland	1
England	7	v	Scotland	0	England	8	v	Ireland	4
England	4	v	S. Africa	1	England	2	v	Germany	1
England	6	v	Wales	1	1966				
England	1	v	Australia	1	England	5	v	Scotland	2
1960					England	2	v	Germany	1
England	3	v	Germany	1	England	2	v	Wales	1
England	4	v	Wales	1	England	3	v	Ireland	0
England	7	v	Scotland	0	1967				
England	4	v	Ireland	1	England	1	v	Wales	0
1961					England	7	v	Ireland	1
England	4	v	Wales	0	England	4	v	Scotland	0
England	4	v	Ireland	2	England	1	v	Holland	1
England	2	v	Holland	1					

World Tournament – Germany – 1967

England	3	v	S. Africa	1
England	1	v	France	0
England	0	v	Australia	0
England	8	v	Argentine	0
England	4	v	Canada	0
England	1	v	Belgium	0

Lawn Tennis

Wimbledon Championships

	Ladies' Singles	Ladies' Doubles
1952	Miss M. C. Connolly	Miss S. J. Fry and Miss D. J. Hart
1953	Miss M. C. Connolly	Miss S. J. Fry and Miss D. J. Hart
1954	Miss M. C. Connolly	Miss A. L. Brough and Mrs W. du Pont
1955	Miss A. L. Brough	Miss A. Mortimer and Miss J. A. Shilock
1956	Miss S. J. Fry	Miss A. Buxton and Miss A. Gibson
1957	Miss A. Gibson	Miss A. Gibson and Miss D. R. Hard
1958	Miss A. Gibson	Miss M. E. Bueno and Miss A. Gibson
1959	Miss M. E. Bueno	Miss J. Arth and Miss D. R. Hard
1960	Miss M. E. Bueno	Miss M. E. Bueno and Miss D. R. Hard
1961	Miss A. Mortimer	Miss K. Hantze and Miss B. J. Moffitt
1962	Mrs J. R. Susman	Miss B. J. Moffitt and Mrs J. R. Susman
1963	Miss M. Smith	Miss M. E. Bueno and Miss D. R. Hard
1964	Miss M. E. Bueno	Miss M. Smith and Miss L. R. Turner
1965	Miss M. Smith	Miss M. E. Bueno and Miss B. J. Moffitt
1966	Mrs L. W. King	Miss M. E. Bueno and Miss N. Richey
1967	Mrs L. W. King	Miss R. Casals and Mrs. L. W. King
1968	Mrs. L. W. King	Miss R. Casals and Mrs. L. W. King

Show Jumping

Queen Elizabeth II Cup Winners

1951　Miss I. Kellett (Eire) *riding* Rusty.
1952　Mrs. G. Rich (UK) *riding* Quicksilver.
1953　Miss M. Delfosse (UK) *riding* Fanny Rosa.
1954　Mlle. J. Bonnaud (France) *riding* Charleston.
1955　Miss D. Palethorpe (UK) *riding* Earlsrath Rambler.
1956　Miss D. Palethorpe (UK) *riding* Earlsrath Rambler.
1957　Miss E. Anderson (UK) *riding* Sunsalve.
1958　Miss P. Smythe (UK) *riding* Mr. Pollard.
1959　Frl. Anna Clement (Germany) *riding* Nico.
1960　Miss S. Cohen (UK) *riding* Clare Castle.
1961　Lady Sarah Fitzalan-Howard (UK) *riding* Oorskiet.
1962　Mrs. B. J. Crago (UK) *riding* Spring Fever.
1963　Miss J. Nash (UK) *riding* Trigger Hill.
1964　Miss G. M. Makin (UK) *riding* Jubilant.
1965　Miss M. Coakes (UK) *riding* Stroller.
1966　Miss A. Roger-Smith (UK) *riding* Havana Royal.
1967　Miss B. Jennaway (UK) *riding* Grey Leg.

Ladies' European Championship

1957	Miss P. Smythe (UK)	1963	Miss P. Smythe (UK)
1958	Signorina G. Serventi (Italy)	1964	No championship
1959	Miss A. Townsend (UK)	1965	Miss M. Coakes (UK)
1960	Miss S. Cohen (UK)	1966	Mlle. J. Lefèbvre (France)
1961	Miss P. Smythe (UK)	1967	Miss K. Kusner (USA)
1962	Miss P. Smythe (UK)		

Swimming

UK Native Records [Ladies]

Event	Holder	Time min.	sec.
100 yards freestyle	D. E. Wilkinson		56·5
110 yards freestyle	A. E. Jackson	1	2·1
220 yards freestyle	E. C. Long	2	16·1
440 yards freestyle	S. E. Williams	4	46·8
880 yards freestyle	S. E. Williams	9	59·8
100 yards breast stroke	E. A. Baxter	1	11·0
110 yards breast stroke	D. A. Harris	1	17·7
220 yards breast stroke	J. Slattery	2	30·6
220 yards breast stroke	J. Slattery	2	49·0
100 yards back stroke	J. A. Franklin	1	1·6
110 yards back stroke	L. K. Ludgrove	1	9·0
220 yards back stroke	J. A. Franklin	2	14·1
220 yards back stroke	L. K. Ludgrove	2	28·5
100 yards butterfly	M. A. Cotterill	1	2·8
110 yards butterfly	E. Tanner	1	7·9
220 yards butterfly	A. Barner	2	36·4
220 yards individual medley	S. H. Ratcliffe	2	34·6
400 yards individual medley	A. Lonsbrough	4	58·0
440 yards individual medley	S. H. Ratcliffe	5	26·7

UK Native Records [Girls]

Event	Holder	Time min.	sec.
100 yards freestyle	A. E. Jackson		57·2
110 yards freestyle	A. E. Jackson	1	2·6

Event	Holder	Time	
		min.	sec.
220 yards freestyle	S. E. Williams	2	17·2
440 yards freestyle	S. E. Williams	4	52·2
880 yards freestyle	S. E. Williams	9	59·8
100 yards back stroke	J. A. Franklin	1	2·2
110 yards back stroke	J. A. Franklin	1	10·3
100 yards breast stroke	D. A. Harris	1	11·4
110 yards breast stroke	A. Radnage	1	19·1
200 yards breast stroke	A. Radnage	2	36·5
220 yards breast stroke	A. Radnage	2	51·0
100 yards butterfly	A. Barner	1	3·8
110 yards butterfly	A. Barner	1	8·8
220 yards individual medley	S. H. Ratcliffe	2	34·6
440 yards individual medley	S. H. Ratcliffe	5	27·4

Channel Swimmers

The distance between Cap Gris Nez in France to Dover in England is some 20 miles, but because of tides a swimmer crossing the Strait has to swim very much farther, the actual distance depending upon when and where he enters the water in relation to the state of the tide, and how long he takes in crossing.

The first Channel swimmer was Capt. Matthew Webb (England), who in 1875 swam from Dover to Calais in 21¾ hours, covering about 40 miles in the effort.

The next swimmer was Thomas Burgess (England), who in 1911 also crossed from Dover to Calais, taking 22 hr. 35 min. Since 1923 the time has been greatly reduced.

The first woman Channel swimmer was Gertrude Ederle (USA), who in 1926 swam from Calais to Dover in 14 hr. 39 min.

Fastest crossings by women:
France to England: Elaine Gray (UK), 10 hr. 24 min. (1967).
England to France: Greta Andersen (USA), 11 hr. 1 min. (1964).
Only woman to cross four times: Greta Andersen (USA).

The Olympic Games

The present series of Olympic Games began in 1896, and Games have been held in the following places: Athens (1896), Paris (1900), St. Louis (1904), London (1908), Stockholm (1912), Antwerp (1920), Paris (1924), Amsterdam (1928), Los Angeles (1932), Berlin (1936), London (1948), Helsinki (1952), Melbourne (1956), Rome (1960), Tokyo (1964).

In the 1956 Games the following events were won by competitors representing the UK: Equestrian Three-Day Event (team win); Swimming, 100 metres back stroke (Judy Grinham); Boxing, flyweight (T. Spinks), lightweight (R. McTaggert); Steeplechase, 3,000 metres (Chris Brasher); Fencing, women's individual foils (G. Sheen).

In the 1960 Games the events won by competitors representing the UK were: 50-kilometre walk (D. Thompson); Swimming, women's 200 metres breast stroke (A. Lonsbrough).

In the 1964 Games the events won by competitors representing the UK were: 20-kilometres walk (K. Matthews); long jump (L. Davies); women's long jump (Mary Rand).

Venue for the 1968 Games: Mexico City.

What shall I do?

How often have you asked yourself this question – on a day when the weather is too bad to go out of doors, on a long journey or when ill in bed? Reading and listening to the radio help to while away some of the time, but these can eventually become boring and one starts looking for other ways of occupying oneself.

This chapter is intended to give briefly some ideas of ways to answer the question at the head of this section. Possible things to do can be divided into six groups: collecting, modelling, needlework, cookery, finding out and playing games just for fun – not that the other five are not enjoyable. These divisions may already suggest to you some ways of passing the time, but if not read on and we shall look at them in a little more detail.

Things to do on a wet day

Collecting

From time to time, most of us try our hands at collecting such things as postage stamps, postmarks, picture postcards, matchbox tops, crests, coins, feathers, shells, leaves or flowers, and a wet day provides an ideal opportunity to sort through new items and put them in their correct place in the collection, and to discard duplicates or poor specimens.

If the weather is still bad when you have done all this, find out more about your chosen hobby – collecting things is more than accumulating objects in a shoe box. That is only the beginning. You will find your collection much more interesting – and your friends will *want* to see it – if you have arranged it neatly, labelled the various items and know something about them.

Magazines and books cover the majority of popular hobbies so have a look for them next time you go to your public library or into your local bookshop. Above all be a knowledgeable collector – not just an accumulator!

Modelling

This section is intended to give you some new ideas, not so much for making models, but for making useful articles – toys and decorations, even presents – from inexpensive materials which are likely to be available in many homes.

Making a mobile. This form of decoration consists basically of one or more wire frames from which you hang fairly light objects. When hung from the ceiling in a good draught, it is fascinating to watch the hanging objects moving in different directions in space – this is a form of Kinetic Art.

One of the simplest forms of mobile can be built up on a wire coat hanger. You could colour halves of egg shells, and hang these by fine thread from the wire frame. Alternatively you can cut shapes – fish or birds or just squares, triangles and circles – from coloured card and attach them to the frame. You will find there is quite a knack in deciding the positions of the objects required to achieve both artistic and physical balance. If you use stiff wire instead of a coat hanger, you will probably find the mobile looks better if the main wire is not hanging from its mid-point, but to do that you will have to balance the weight carefully.

Carving. Have you ever tried whittling? All you need is a sharp knife and a piece of freshly cut wood. Make thin rather than deep cuts even if you want to halve the thickness of your stick and *always* push the knife away from you. Start off by making something simple, such as a paper knife. You could even make a collection of such knives carefully rubbed down and oiled to show the grains of different woods.

When you become more proficient you can try your hand at whittling solid shapes – such as animals and birds. A forked stick will provide the extra thickness you will need for such objects. Once you start you will find certain pieces of stick suggest particular shapes to whittle. If you cannot find any suitable fresh-cut sticks on a wet day you can always try carving cheap tablets of soap or modelling with Plaster of Paris or clay.

Paper mâché is another useful material for making all manner of things from heads of puppets, to trays, bowls and relief maps of hilly areas. You will need old newspaper, a large bowl, some wall-paper paste, a paste brush, water, a base upon which to build and some white shelf paper.

First you tear the paper into small pieces and put them into a bowl of water. While the paper is getting thoroughly soaked, make the wall-paper paste. Once the pieces of paper are really wet you are ready to start. Spread paste evenly over the base, then squeeze out as much water as possible from the pieces of paper and slowly lay these out over the base. Take care to smooth each piece out carefully avoiding creases and bubbles. Gradually build up the thickness, pasting between each layer of paper.

If you want some parts to be thicker than others – if for instance you are making a head for a puppet – the nose and cheeks will need to be built up, while if you have chosen a relief map hills need the same treatment. When your object is thick enough and you have achieved the right shape finish off with two layers of pieces of very wet white paper (shelf paper will do admirably). Once you have completed this stage you must leave the object in a warm place. Do not try lifting the object off its base until it is thoroughly dry, otherwise the shape will be lost. Finally finish it off with paint or varnish.

Keeping a sketch book

You may not think that a wet day is the best time to start a sketch book, but it will give you the opportunity to try your skill and also to experiment with different materials. Try using charcoal, chalk, felt and other types of pen, instead of pencil.

Remember that sketches are quick jottings rather than finished drawings. Try to capture the main lines of movement – do not worry about details. Copy the cartoonist's technique of using just a few bold lines. Possible subjects for sketching on a wet day include a corner of your room, a view from your window, dog (or cat) coming in from the rain (plenty of movement as he shakes himself), or try to sketch from memory your street, the entrance to your school, a corner of the park or a view of a local beauty spot. Take the latter sketches with you next time you go to the place and see how good your memory is.

Needlework
A wet day provides an ideal opportunity to try out or improve your knitting, embroidery or crocheting (*see pages 105 to 113*). If you have imagination and scraps of material you might like to make shoe pads or possibly oven mittens or a patch-work apron. With scraps of wool you could knit or crochet squares which you can sew together to make cushion covers or perhaps a baby's shawl or doll's blanket.

With a few 'dolly' pegs and scraps of material or crêpe paper you can make a whole family of peg dolls, from grandfather down to baby.

Cookery
If your mother is not too busy perhaps she will let you experiment in the kitchen, trying out some of the recipes on pages 90 to 96. You may even want to have a go at toffee making!

Finding out
A visit to the public library or a museum (if your town has one) is an ideal way of passing an hour or two on a wet day and can start you off on a new hobby or interest. In towns which do not have a museum you will often find that the public library has a small display case of relics which have been found in the neighbourhood. Find out about them. From what period do they date? What did the people of that time do? You are now getting interested in either archaeology or local history – borrow a book about one or the other from the library and find out more. Are there any statues in the market place of your own town – or the nearest large town? If so, find out what made these people famous. If yours is an old town, find out when the old houses were built. In the older parts of the town modern shop fronts may have been put on to old houses, so look at the upper floors from the other side of the street. Notice the different building materials used.

If you do not want to go out, you could plan your next expedition for

126

when the weather improves and if you are not very proficient at map reading, you have a splendid opportunity to learn the mapping signs. A good way of doing this is to draw the various signs on to small pieces of white card – one sign to each – and use the cards to play a form of 'snap'. You could try drawing from memory a sketch map of your neighbourhood.

Things to do on a long journey

However beautiful the scenery may be, sooner or later you will probably get bored with watching it aimlessly. As with many other activities, a journey can be much more interesting – and the time pass more quickly – if you have definite objectives; for instance, to record various landmarks along the route. So before you start the journey, whether you are going by coach, private car, train or by air, find out your route and plot it on a map. Notice whether you are likely to pass through any interesting places on the way – you will then know in advance some of the sites to look for.

Here are some of the things you can watch for. You will have a greater chance of seeing these items of interest if you are going by road as you will go right through the centres of some towns, but others can be seen equally well from a train.

1   white horses and other figures cut out on the side of chalk downs; stone circles, mounds and other relics of the early inhabitants of Britain;
2   old houses and cottages – estimate how old they are from their shape and the materials from which they are made;
3   stocks, pillories, whipping posts and ducking stools which were used for punishing offenders years ago are sometimes to be seen on village greens;
4   notice the different types of boundaries – hedges, fences and dry stone or slate walls – used to divide fields. The choice depends upon materials available locally and how exposed the countryside is to wind.
5   what crops are growing and animals grazing in the fields? Learn the difference between the various breeds of cattle, pigs and sheep. Watch out also for wild life – ponies, deer, hares and rabbits.
6   notice the quaint names and signs outside country inns – also the pictorial sign boards beside the roads as you enter some towns and villages. Try going through the alphabet with inn names – Angel, Bell, Cartwright, Dolphin.

Looking for things of this sort can be much more fun if you have several companions with you on the journey, then the first person to spot any item scores a point. Give bonus points for the rarer items.

Parts of railway journeys can be less interesting – particularly if you are going through cuttings or the industrial outskirts of large towns, though you can always try estimating the speed of the train by counting the number of telegraph poles which you pass in a minute. The poles are planted at 50-yard intervals, so that if the train is travelling at 60 miles per hour (1 mile/min.) you will pass 35 poles (1,760 ÷ 50) in one minute. You can work out other speeds from this information.

Alternatively, you can find your own amusement in the train – for instance, see how many words you can write down in, say five minutes, from the letters of a long word such as archaeology. You can also make up a chain story – one person starts and part way through an exciting episode, breaks off, and someone else has to continue.

Further Reading

Junior Pears Leisure Book (Pelham).
Something to Do, Septima (Penguin).
Know the Game Photography (Educational Productions).
Know the Game Stamp Collecting (Educational Productions).
I-Spy Archaeology (Dickens Press).
I-Spy in the Hedgrow (Dickens Press).
I-Spy on a Car Journey (Dickens Press).
I-Spy on a Train Journey (Dickens Press).